THE ART OF
T'SHUVA

The Teachings of
HaRav Avraham Yitzhak HaCohen Kook

THE ART
OF
T'SHUVA

Commentary by

Rabbi David Samson and Tzvi Fishman

Shorashim • Jerusalem

For information: Shorashim - Fishman, 19 Shoshana St., Apt. 8,
                Jerusalem, Israel 96149
e-mail: fishman11@bezeqint.net

Computer typeset by Moshe Kaplan

Printed in Israel

We gratefully acknowledge the generosity of Rubin and Lib Paz, Dr. Irving Moskowitz, Seymour Schneiderman, Dr. Rubin and Mandy Brecher. Their support was instrumental in bringing this project to fruition.

The writing of this book was inspired by the memory of our dear friend, Rabbi Pesach Jaffe זצ"ל, a master of the t'shuva experience and a paragon of the teachings of Rabbi Kook.

TABLE OF CONTENTS

LETTER OF BLESSING

HaRav Avraham Elkanah Kahana Shapira, *Shlita*
Rosh Yeshiva, Mercaz HaRav, Jerusalem
Former Chief Rabbi of Israel

The hearts of HaRav David Samson and the writer, Tzvi Fishman, have been moved to translate and explain the writings of HaRav Kook, זצ״ל, on the subject of t'shuva, for our English-speaking brothers. For many years, HaRav Samson was a student of HaRav Tzvi Yehuda Kook, זצ״ל, the son of HaRav Kook. Under his tutelage, he learned the book, *Orot HaT'shuva.* Also during his many years in our yeshiva, HaRav Samson learned about t'shuva with me in my classes on the *Laws of T'shuva* of the Rambam.

The authors are already well-known for their previous books which were gladly received by our English-speaking brothers. These books have brought many closer to Torah and to the Land of Israel. They serve as brightly lit pathways to the writings and thoughts of our teacher, HaRav Kook, זצ״ל, for the many people who cannot understand the original texts.

In our generation, when millions of our people do not know the Hebrew language, and when myriads long to embrace the path of t'shuva, there is special importance in making the writings of HaRav Kook on t'shuva available to English speakers in a clear and comprehensible fashion.

Therefore, I bless the authors with the blessing of a Kohen, in everything material and spiritual, that the Almighty will help them be successful in spreading the teachings of HaRav, ל״צז, and be successful in bringing our people closer to Hashem and to Torah.

May it be G-d's will that we merit a complete redemption, as our Sages say, *Great is t'shuva for it brings the redemption close, as it says, And a redeemer shall come to Zion, and he will restore the sinners of Yaacov,* speedily, in our time, Amen.

With the blessings of Torah,
HaRav Avraham Shapira

Adar, 5759

PREFACE

Generally, t'shuva is thought of as a religious way of getting one's life together — a system of do's and don'ts, separating right from wrong, good deeds from bad.

While this is certainly an aspect of t'shuva, the source of t'shuva is something much deeper. T'shuva is more than a scorecard of pluses and minuses, leading to a reward up in heaven.

The magnificance of t'shuva lies in its depth. Rabbi Kook writes that, "The foundation of t'shuva is an accounting of man's state in the world. The roots of this accounting are higher than the accounting itself, just as the theory of numbers is above the numbers themselves."[1]

T'shuva is something above a simple accounting of the rights and wrongs in a person's life. T'shuva is a spiritual enterprise which encompasses all of creation. **T'shuva is the expression of the world's existential yearning to come closer to G-d.**

It sometimes happens in the world of Orthodox Judaism that

1. *Orot HaT'shuva*, 16:1.

people can focus on the arena of do's and don'ts, and get bogged down in the precepts. If this happens, the observance of the commandments can become mechanical. One can forget to delve into the deeper realities behind the external deeds. Because one does not see the roots of a tree, one can forget that the roots are keeping the tree upright. The root of Judaism is cleaving to G-d.[2] This is what lies at the foundation of the commandments.[3] It is a feeling,[4] a vision,[5] a life project,[6] a joy.[7]

People who are only involved in the dry mechanics of Judaism sometimes feel that life is lacking real substance and inspiration.[8] They want to feel close to G-d, and to experience a more spiritual high. Not having delved into the deeper understandings of Judaism, they do not realize that the practical *mitzvot* and the Divine "high" which they are seeking actually go together. G-d is to be found in the *mitzvot* themselves, and in all of the details of life.[9] This is the beauty of Judaism. G-d is with you every moment of your life, in everything you do.[10]

2. Deuteronomy, 30:20.

3. Joshua, 22:5.

4. *Kuntres HaHitpa'alut*, beginning of Forward, by HaRav Dov Ber, the son of HaRav Shneur Zalman of Liadi.

5. *Berachot* 34b, beginning, *All the prophets....*

6. Rambam, *Sefer HaMitzvot*, 6.

7. *Messilat Yesharim*, Chapter One, by HaRav Moshe Chaim Luzzato, beginning *To delight in Hashem.*

8. See *Lights On Orot*, Chapter Two, by Rabbi David Samson and Tzvi Fishman, Torat Eretz Yisrael Publications, Jerusalem.

9. *Messilat Yesharim*, Chapter Two.

10. Proverbs, 3:6. See the commentary of the Malbim there.

Rabbi Kook teaches that this deeper understanding of Judaism can be discovered through the wonders of t'shuva. It is only through returning to G-d, in all aspects of our beings, that each person, and all of mankind, will find true joy and salvation from the straitjacket of practicalism which is suffocating the world today.[11]

Undertaking a commentary of Rabbi Kook's writings is never an easy assignment. While this is our fourth book on Rabbi Kook, his writings on t'shuva, *Orot HaT'shuva*, presented us with our most formidable task to date. His deeply poetic and visionary style defies simple, straightforward exegesis. Certainly, in explaining Rabbi Kook's teachings in a popular manner, we have missed much of the depth. We have also not ventured to comment on all of his writings on t'shuva. This book is more of a primer, a general guide to Rabbi Kook's thoughts on the topic. Readers proficient in Hebrew are invited to tackle the original Hebrew themselves.

We would like to thank our rabbis at Rabbi Kook's Mercaz HaRav Yeshiva in Jerusalem for helping to unlock the mysteries of *Orot Hat'shuva*. First and foremost were the classes of Rabbi Kook's only son, HaRav Tzvi Yehuda Kook, זצ״ל, the Rosh Yeshiva. We have also gleaned added insight from Rabbi Tzvi Tau, *shlita*; Rabbi Shlomo Aviner, *shlita*; Rabbi Yehoshua Zuckerman, *shlita*; and Rabbi Dov Begon, *shlita*. We have also relied on the notes and sources of Rabbi Yaacov Filber, found in his excellent Hebrew book, *Commentary and Sources to Orot HaT'shuva*, published by the Research Institute for the Writings of Rabbi Avraham Yitzhak HaCohen Kook, Jerusalem. In translating sec-

---

11.   *Orot*, pg. 84, Section 44, HaRav Avraham Yitzhak HaCohen Kook.

tions of Rabbi Kook's writings, we have tried to capture the general teaching, rather than to present a rigid, word-for-word rendition. For interested readers, a very useful translation of *Orot HaT'shuva* can be found in the book, *Abraham Isaac Kook*, by Ben Zion Bokser, in the series, *Classics of Western Spirituality*, Paulist Press, New York. Another translation, *Lights of Return*, by Rabbi Alter Metzger, was published by Yeshiva University Press.

Once again, we would like to pay tribute to Rabbi Yehuda Hazani, זצ"ל, who inspired us to work on the *Torat Eretz Yisrael* series. Michael Lerner and Danny Rose labored conscientiously on the manuscript to prepare it for printing. Finally, we would like to thank our dear friend and colleague, Rabbi Moshe Kaplan, for his professional editing and layout work on the book.

RABBI KOOK'S INTRODUCTION

to the book

OROT HAT'SHUVA

"For some time now, I have been struggling with an inner battle. A powerful force is impelling me to speak on the subject of t'shuva. All of my thoughts are concentrated only on this. The greatest part of the Torah and of life is devoted to the matter of t'shuva. All of the hopes of the individual and of the community are founded upon it. T'shuva is a Divine commandment which is both the easiest, since the thought of t'shuva is considered t'shuva in itself,[1] and on the other hand, it is the hardest of the *mitzvot*, since its essence has not yet been fully revealed in the world and in life.

"I find myself constantly thinking and wanting to speak exclusively about t'shuva. Much has been written on the subject of t'shuva in the Torah, in the Prophets, and in the writings of the

---

1. *Kiddushin* 49B.

1

Sages, but for our generation, the matters are still obscure and require clarification. Literature, which can be found wherever life and song abound, has not penetrated at all this wonderous treasure of life, the treasure of t'shuva. In truth, literature has not even begun to gaze upon it, to know its content and value, not even regarding its poetic side which is a fountain of infinite creativity. And accordingly, our literature has certainly not examined its practical side, especially concerning the modern world in which we live.

"My inner essence compels me to speak about t'shuva. And and yet I myself am taken aback by my own thoughts. Am I worthy enough to speak about t'shuva? The great souls of the past wrote about t'shuva, the prophets, the holiest Sages, and the greatest masters of piety; how can I venture to join their ranks? However, no shortcoming in the world can discourage me from fulfilling my inner claim. I am driven to speak about t'shuva. Particularly about its literary and practical sides, to understand its meaning for our generation, and to actualize its expression, in the life of the individual and in the life of the nation as a whole."

כתב-יד קדשו של מרן הרב זצ"ל

אורות התשובה, פרק ט' סעיף א'

Original manuscript page from *OROT HAT'SHUVA*

And you shall return to the L-rd your G-d, and shall obey His voice according to all that I command you this day, you and your children, with all your heart and with all your soul. Then the L-rd your G-d will return your captivity and have compassion on you, and will return and gather you from all the nations amongst whom the L-rd your G-d has scattered you. If your outcasts be at the utmost parts of heaven, from there will the L-rd your G-d gather you, and from there will He fetch you. And the L-rd your G-d will bring you into the Land which your fathers possessed, and you shall possess it. And He will do you good and multiply you more than your fathers. And the L-rd your G-d will circumcise your heart and the heart of your seed, to love the L-rd your G-d with all your heart and with all your soul, that you may live.

Deuteronomy 30:2-6

Chapter One

THE SECRET OF HAPPINESS

BE HAPPY

Dear Reader — if you are looking to be happy, creative, in harmony with G-d and with the universe, Rabbi Kook has the answer — t'shuva.

For Rabbi Kook, t'shuva is a concept much deeper than the common understanding of repentance. It is much more than a penitence over sins and the remorse a person must feel when he strays from the pathways of goodness and truth. While t'shuva includes these factors, the phenomenon of t'shuva spreads out over all of the universe, bringing harmony and perfection to all of existence.

RETURN TO THE SOURCE

While t'shuva is normally translated as penitence or repentance, the root of the Hebrew word t'shuva means "return."

T'shuva is a return to the source, to one's roots, to one's deepest inner self. Rabbi Kook writes:

"When one forgets the essence of one's soul; when one distracts his mind from seeing the true nature of his own inner life, everything becomes doubtful and confused. The principal t'shuva, which immediately lights up the darkness, is for a person to return to himself, to the root of his soul. Then he will immediately return to G-d, to the Soul of all souls. And he will continue to stride higher and higher in holiness and purity. This is true for an individual, a nation, for all of mankind, and for the perfection of all existence...."[1]

Anything which is a return to the pure, original, natural state, whether it be physical, moral, or spiritual, is a part of t'shuva. As Rabbi Kook develops his ideas about t'shuva, he speaks not only about the individual, but about the Jewish nation as a whole. T'shuva encompasses the nation of Israel, and more. All of humanity is destined for perfection and upliftment.[2] Rabbi Kook even writes about the t'shuva of the heavens and earth — when the bark of a tree will be as edible as its fruit,[3] and when the moon will return to its original size, as big and bright as the

1. *Orot HaT'shuva*, 15:10. See also, 12:8a, "T'shuva is basically a movement of returning to one's original state, to the root of life and higher existence, in their wholeness, without restriction and constriction, in their most exalted spiritual ideals, as they are illumined by the pure, brilliant supernal light." Also, *Orot HaT'shuva*, Ohr Etzion Edition, Appendix, pg. 149.

2. *Orot HaT'shuva*, 17:1.

3. Rabbi Kook is referring to the Midrash which teaches that the bark of a tree and its fruit were originally to have the same taste. *Bereshit Rabbah*, 5:9.

sun.[4] In effect, t'shuva is the force which pushes all physical and spiritual worlds towards completion.[5]

One can readily understand that to reach fulfillment and happiness, a person must be his true self. In modern times, this basic understanding has been corrupted into a "do your own thing" attitude. Rabbi Kook is advocating a deeper, inner search, far beyond the surface passions and emotions which often lead people to express their every desire and lust. Rabbi Kook understands that the individual, and all of existence, has a deeper, spiritual source. In the depths of this ever-pure realm, our true essence lies. A person who makes the inward journey of t'shuva comes to encounter his soul and the Creator who gave it. As Rabbi Kook writes:

"It is only through the great truth of returning to oneself that the individual, the nation, the world, all of the worlds, and all of existence, will return to its Maker, to be illuminated by the light of life."[6]

---

4. The Midrash teaches that the sun and moon were the same size at Creation. This is indicated by the Biblical verse describing how G-d created the two great lights. The verse continues to state that the greater light was to rule the day, and the lesser light to rule the night. The Sages tell us that in punishment for wanting to rule the heavens alone, the moon was made smaller in size than the sun. *Bereshit Rabbah*, 6:3. See also *Rashi*, Genesis, 1:16.

5. *Orot HaT'shuva*, 4:2.

6. Ibid, 15:10.

Throughout history, man has been searching to discover the driving force of life. To a capitalist, money makes the world go around. To a romanticist, love is what impassions mankind. Freudians claim that man's unconscious desires and libido are to blame. Peering into a microscope, a modern physicist declares that atoms and neutrons cause the world to spin. For biologists, the uniting power resides in strands of DNA.

When Rabbi Kook gazes into the inner workings of the soul, the soul of the individual, and the soul of the world, he sees that the force behind all existence is t'shuva.

THE AGE OF ANXIETY

It is no secret that there is great darkness, confusion, and pain in the world. Bookstores are filled with self-help books on how to be happy. Layman's guides to psychology line shelf after shelf. Our generation has been called "the age of anxiety."[7] People often live out their lives plagued with depression, sickness, a sense of unfulfillment and constant unrest. Psychiatrists, psychologists, and humanists like Freud, Jung, Adler, Horney, Fromm, May, Erikson, Dr. Dryer, and dozens of others have become the prophets of the moment, proposing dozens of theories to explain man's existential dilemmas. Whether it is because we suffer from an Oedipus complex, or from a primal anxiety at having been separated from the womb, from sexual repression, or from the trauma of death, mankind is beset with neuroses. Vials of valium and an assortment of anti-depressants and "uppers" can be found in the medicine cabinets of the very best homes. Not to mention

---

7. See the book, *The Age of Anxiety* by Rollo May, Harper and Row Publishers.

the twenty-four-hour bombardment of work, television, computer games, discos, and drugs which people use to blot out the never-ending angst that they feel.

The psychologist, Erich Fromm, in his book, *Psychoanalysis and Religion* describes an interesting photograph which captures the average man's pain:

"It is proclaimed by many voices that our way of life makes us happy. But how many people of these times are happy? It is interesting to remember a casual shot in *Life* magazine some time ago of a group of people waiting on a street corner for the green light. What was so remarkable and shocking about this picture was that these people who all looked stunned and frightened had not witnessed a dreadful accident but, as the text had to explain, were merely average citizens going about their business."[8]

Fromm continues and states: "We pretend that our life is based on a solid foundation and ignore the shadows of uneasiness, anxiety and confusion which never leave us."[9]

Rabbi Kook understands all of this darkness and anguish. He sees its source not in external causes, not in the traumas of childhood, nor in the pressures to conform to behavioral norms. He looks beyond social, cultural, psychological, sexual, and family dynamics to shed spiritual light on the world's confusion and pain.

8.   Erich Fromm, *Psychoanalysis and Religion*, pg. 3, Yale University Press, New Haven.
9.   Ibid.

"What is the cause of melancholy? The answer is the over-abundance of evil deeds, evil character traits, and evil beliefs on the soul. The souls deep sensitivity feels the bitterness which these cause, and it draws back, frightened and depressed."[10]

"All depression stems from sin, and t'shuva comes to light the soul and transforms the depression to joy. The source of the general pain in the world derives from the overall moral pollution of the universe, resulting from the sins of nations and individuals, and from the hidden sin of the earth, which was exposed through the transgression of man."[11]

If Rabbi Kook were to have studied the *Life* magazine photograph of the tense, unhappy people on the street corner who were waiting to cross the street, he would have suggested a far deeper reason for their anxiety than any psychologist could propose. A deeper reason, and a novel cure:

"Every sin causes a special anxiety on the spirit, which can only be erased by t'shuva. According to the depth of the t'shuva, the anxiety itself is transformed into inner security and courage. The outer manifestation of anxiety which is caused by transgression can be discerned in the lines of the face, in a person's movements, in the voice, in behavior, and one's handwriting, in the manner of speaking and one's language, and above all, in

10. *Orot HaT'shuva*, 14:6. See also, 8:11, "Sins are the root of melancholy."
11. *Orot HaT'shuva*, 14:7. Once again, Rabbi Kook is referring to the earth's failure to produce trees with edible barks. When Adam was cursed for his sin, the earth was cursed with him. Their sins brought exile and pain to the world. *Bereshit Rabbah*, 5:9. See also, *Orot HaT'shuva*, 6:7, and Chapter Ten of this book.

writing, in the development of ideas and their presentation."[12]

The melancholy and anxiety haunting mankind is not a result of the "trauma of birth," but of a spiritual separation much deeper — the separation from G-d.

"I see how transgressions act as a barrier against the brilliant Divine light which shines on every soul, and they darken and cast a shadow upon the soul."[13]

The remedy is t'shuva — for the individual, the community, and for the world. **Rabbi Kook teaches that to discover true inner joy, every person, and all of Creation, must return to the Source of existence and forge a living connection to G-d.**

The paperbacks on personal improvement, psychology, and self-help which line bookstore shelves, contain many useful insights and tips. After all, man is influenced by a wide gamut of factors dating back even before his conception, through his time in the womb, his childhood years, and spanning the many life passages each of us face. Rabbi Kook reveals that in addition to all of the fashionable theories and cures, on a far deeper level, there is a spiritual phenomenon of wonderous beauty, like a

---

12. *Orot HaT'shuva*, 8:13. The Talmud, *Berachot* 60A, relates that a student was walking with his teacher through the market in Jerusalem. Seeing that the student was fearful, the teacher called him a sinner, quoting the verse, Isaiah, 33:14, *The sinners in Zion are afraid.*
13. *Orot HaT'shuva*, 7:5.

butterfly enclosed in a cacoon, waiting to soar free. This is the light and healing wonder of t'shuva.

Chapter Two

THREE STAGES OF T'SHUVA

Rabbi Kook begins his exploration of t'shuva by describing its three basic phases.[1] He tells us that a person seeking happiness in life should have:

1) a healthy body and mind

2) a healthy orientation to religious belief

3) an idealistic aspiration to be in line with G-d's plan for the universe.

"We discover t'shuva in three different spheres: t'shuva related to nature; t'shuva related to faith; and t'shuva related to intellect."[2]

---

1.   *Orot HaT'shuva*, 1.
2.   Ibid.

GETTING IN SHAPE

The concept of t'shuva, which goes beyond a mere religious mending of one's ways to encompass the perfection of all of Creation, begins with the simple advice to be healthy. We mentioned that t'shuva is essentially a return to one's roots. To do this, a person must first return to his natural physical being, to his natural physical self. **To reach inner peace and harmony with the world, an individual must first have a healthy body.**

In our days, where health-food stores and sports clubs abound, this simple teaching is known to almost everyone. A healthy body is the basis of all creative endeavor. What is new, however, is that Rabbi Kook sees this as part of the process of t'shuva. Being in good shape is an important factor not only in attaining personal well-being, but also in forging a connection to G-d.[3]

"Physical t'shuva encompasses all of the transgressions against the laws of nature, and against the laws of morality and Torah which relate to the laws of nature. In the end, every bad habit must cause illness and pain. Because of this, the individual and the community suffer greatly. After a person realizes that his own improper behavior is responsible for his life's physical decline, he thinks to correct the situation, to return to the laws of life, to adhere to the laws of nature, of morality, and of Torah, so that he may return to live revitalized by all of life's vigor."[4]

3. See, Rambam, *Mishne Torah, Laws of De'ot*, 4:1.
4. *Orot HaT'shuva*, 1.

A person is healthy when all of his metabolism is functioning in the proper natural balance. A person in tune with his body's correct internal workings is able to be correctly aligned with the world. While this sounds like some Eastern mystical teaching, it is simply good advice. To hook up with the spiritual channels connecting heaven and earth, a person must first be in a healthy physical state. For instance, one of the basic requirements of prophecy is a strong, healthy body.[5] Physical and spiritual health go together. The Rambam, who worked as a physician when he was not studying Torah, has systematically detailed in his writings the rules of healthy living, stressing the importance of exercise, proper diet, and bodily care as a prerequisite to keeping the Torah.[6]

Today, everyone seems to have a battery of doctors. People cannot seem to do without an assortment of pills. Medical clinics are filled up months in advance. Yet the natural state of a man is to be healthy. Physical ailment, lethargy, and being overweight are all signs that the body is in need of repair. Sometimes the remedy is medicine. Sometimes a proper diet. Sometimes rest and relaxation are the cure.

Rabbi Kook's call to a state of natural well-being has been partly answered in our generation. Today, there is a vast world industry in being natural. We have natural foods, natural organic vegetables and fruits, natural whole wheat bread, natural herbal teas and medicines, natural clothes, natural childbirth, and an

---

5. *Mishne Torah*, Foundations of Torah, 7:1.
6. Ibid, *Laws of De'ot*, Chapter Four. See also the letter of the Rambam written to King Aftzel, the son of Tzalach a'Din, reprinted by Mossad HaRav Kook under the title *Hanhagat HaBriyut*.

assortment of back-to-nature lifestyles. In the past, it was written on food labels which ingredients were included. Now it is often written which ingredients are NOT INCLUDED: no preservatives, no additives, no salt, no carbohydrates, no artificial coloring, and the like.

In line with this return-to-Eden existence, Rabbi Kook teaches that when a person corrects an unhealthy habit, he or she is doing t'shuva. It turns out that gyms and health clubs from California to Miami are filled with people doing t'shuva. If you are riding an exercise bike to get back into shape, you are coming closer to G-d. Tennis players are doing t'shuva. In Las Vegas, even though the morals of the health-conscious people in aerobics classes may be bent out of shape, they too are engaged in the beginnings of t'shuva.

Accordingly, if a person stops smoking, he is engaging in repentance. If a fat person goes on a diet, he is embarked on a course of personal perfection and *tikun*. When a teenager who is addicted to Pepsi begins to drink fruit juice instead, he is returning to a healthier state. In place of caffeine, his blood will be carrying vitamins throughout all of his system. In the language of the Rambam, this person is replacing a food which merely tastes good, for one that is beneficial to the human metabolism.[7] As he explains, a person should always eat what is healthy and not merely foods that give his taste buds a lift. Interestingly, the Rambam's guide to healthy living,[8] written generations ago, reads like the newest best-seller on the market.

---

7. *Laws of De'ot*, 5:1, *Moreh Nevuchim*, Part Three, Chapter 35:13 (Kapach edition).
8. *Hanhagat HaBriyut*, loc cit.

It is important to note that while physical wellbeing is a basic rule of good living, the injunction to be healthy is a principle of Torah. We are called upon to *carefully guard your life*.[9] This is a warning to avoid needless danger and to watch over our health. Inflicting any kind of physical damage on oneself (like excessive cigarette smoking) is forbidden.[10] The Rambam explains: "Having a whole and healthy body is part and parcel of serving G-d, for it is impossible to have understanding and wisdom in the matter of knowing the Creator if a man is ill. Therefore one must avoid things which damage the body and to habituate oneself with things promoting health."[11]

Toward the end of the book *Orot HaT'shuva*, Rabbi Kook teaches that t'shuva is bound up with personal strength and valor.[12] Man was created to be a strong, active creature. This is true not only for athletes, but for spiritually enlightened people as well. The holy men of the Torah possessed not only great personal attributes and wisdom, but also great physical prowess. Though Yaacov spent all of his youth studying Torah, he could lift up a huge boulder when needed.[13] The "little" shepherd boy David was able to overcome lions and bears.[14] And the holy spirit (*Ruach HaKodesh*) which marked Samson's life was not only wisdom, but incredible physical brawn.[15]

---

9. Deut. 4:9, Rambam, *Laws of Rotze'ach and Shmirat HaNefesh* 11:4.
10. *Baba Kama*, 91B; Rambam, *Laws of Wounds and Damage*, 5:1; *Iggrot Moshe, Even HaEzer* 4:76; *Tzitz Eliezer*, 15:39.
11. Rambam, *Laws of De'ot*, 4:1.
12. *Orot HaT'shuva*, 16:4.
13. Genesis, 29:10.
14. Samuel, Book One, 17:34-36.
15. Judges, 14:6; 14:19; 15:14-15. *Moreh Nevuchim*, Part Two, Chapter 45.

Rabbi Kook writes that a person must do t'shuva for physical weaknesses and their consequences.[16] For instance, a person who is overweight and easily tired may lack the energy to perform the commandments with the proper enthusiasm, or he may feel too weak to resist bodily temptations. His fatigue may interfere with his Torah learning and prayer. In G-d's service, a strong body and a strong mind go hand-in-hand.

Rabbi Kook explains that a weakening of the will is due in large measure to a lack of physical energy and strength.[17] When a person's willpower is weak, he can fall into many bad habits. As part of his overall mending, he must improve his physical health, as well as his moral and spiritual worlds.

A POWERFUL BODY AND SOUL

Interestingly, Rabbi Kook was condemned by certain ultra-Orthodox groups who belonged to the Old Settlement in Jerusalem when he extolled the virtues of exercise and a healthy physique. In his classic work, *Orot*, Rabbi Kook writes that the exercise of young Jews in *Eretz Yisrael*, in order to strengthen their bodies to become mighty sons to the nation, adds overall strength to the Jewish people, which enables the righteous to bring more Divine light into the world.[18]

"When young people engage in sport to strengthen their physical capabilities and morale for the sake of increasing the overall strength of the nation..., this holy endeavor raises the Di-

16. *Orot HaT'shuva*, 14:13.
17. *Orot HaT'shuva*, 14:20.
18. *Orot, Orot HaTechiyah*, pg. 80, para. 34.

vine Presence ever higher, just as it is exalted by the songs and praises sung by David, King of Israel, in the Book of Psalms...."[19]

Upon hearing this comparison between sport and the Psalms of King David, the ultra-Orthodox community in Jerusalem vehemently attacked Rabbi Kook. They were afraid that any praise of the secular Zionists could lead to a crumbling of barriers between the holy and the profane. In addition to that very real concern, their negative attitude toward physical strength can be seen as having evolved from the miserable state of the Jew in the ghetto. In the *Galut*, Diaspora Jews were helpless against the oppression of the gentiles. A philosophy developed whereby a Jew was supposed to look solely to G-d for salvation and rescue. The Jews were so outnumbered, how could they fight? Physical prowess was meaningless.[20] A Jew had to rely solely on Torah and prayer. While that might have been true in the Diaspora, with the return of the Jewish people to Israel, physical strength became a necessity if the Jews were to successfully settle the land and defend Jewish settlements against hostile neighbors.

In the generation of national revival, as the Jewish nation returns to its homeland, a new type of religious Jew must appear to take up the challenge. Rabbi Kook writes in *Orot*:

"Our physical demand is great. We need a healthy body. Through our intense preoccupation with spirituality, we forgot the holiness of the body. We neglected bodily health and

19. Ibid.
20. *Duties of the Heart*, Gate 8, 3:25.

strength. We forgot that we have holy flesh, no less than our holy spirit. We abandoned practical life, and negated our physical senses, and that which is connected to the tangible physical reality, out of a fallen fear,[21] due to a lack of faith in the holiness of the land...."[22]

In fact, it is the revival of the nation's physical strength which brings about a renewed spiritual strengthening.

"All of our t'shuva will only succeed if it will be, along with its spiritual splendor, also a physical t'shuva which produces healthy blood, healthy flesh, firm, mighty bodies, and a flaming spirit spreading over powerful muscles. Through the power of the sanctified flesh, the weakened soul will shine forth — like the dead's physical resurrection."[23]

Jews, religious or not religious, are not to be "*nebechs*" or weaklings whom everyone can push around. We need not be ashamed of our bodies. We must be strong to learn *Gemara*, and strong to build the Land.

In other words, if Jews do not start planting fruit trees in Israel, then the harvest of fruit, the surest sign of redemption,[24] is not going to happen. Rabbi Kook saw that the physical re-

---

21. A "fallen fear" means a fear of G-d that does not include the material world within the scope of holiness.
22. *Orot, Orot HaTechiya,* pg. 80, para. 33.
23. Ibid.
24. *Sanhedrin* 98A.

settlement of Zion, even by secular Jews, was a great act of t'shuva, of returning the nation to its roots.[25]

Thus our first step on the journey of t'shuva is physical health, both for the individual and for the nation. And truly, all over the world, people are jogging their way back to G-d. Once their bodies are in shape, the next step is to change the music in their Walkman headphones to a holier sounding tape.

PSYCHIC HEALTH

The second category of natural t'shuva has to do with the psychic and moral state of man. Rabbi Kook writes:

"A more inner stage of natural t'shuva applies to the psychological and spiritual state. This is commonly known as 'pangs of conscience.' Man has a natural inclination to pursue a path of righteousness. When he strays from the way and falls into sin, if his spiritual sense has not been totally corrupted, this sense of morality will cause unease in his heart, and he will suffer pain. He will hurry to return and correct what has been perverted, to the point where he feels that the transgression has been erased."[26]

This second aspect of natural t'shuva forms the basis of a great deal of Western literature. Man's struggle with the warring sides of his inner nature has provided fertile ground for writers

25. *Orot HaT'shuva*, 17:2, "The revival of the desire of the nation as a whole to return to its Land, to its true identity, to its spirit, and to its character — in truth, the light of t'shuva is shining in this."
26. *Orot HaT'shuva*, 1.

such as Dostoyevski, Tolstoy, Hugo, Dickens, Shakespeare, Balzac, Hardy, and Joyce. Kant, the philosopher, maintained that mankind has a natural tendency toward morality. Psychologists have written innumerable treatises on the subject of moral conscience. To all of them, it was clear that conscience played a key role in man's inner psyche.

By nature, people are generally good. They enjoy helping others and doing good deeds. When a person does bad things, he usually suffers remorse. Rabbi Kook says that this tendency of man drives him to be a better person. When the many powerful forces of life cause a person to stray from the paths of righteousness and goodness, the person will want to cease his lowly behavior and return to a loftier plane. Bothered by the inner voice of his conscience, he longs to rectify his wrongdoing. This call parallels his body's demand to be healthy. Both the body and soul have built-in alarm systems which sound a warning when a person strays too far from the dictates of proper living. As long as this inner sensitivity is still intact, the mechanism of t'shuva promises recovery and rebirth. Inspired by the call to return to a life of physical and moral health, a person can be freed from the malaise of the past. Recommitted to a path of healthy, righteous living, he discovers the happiness he had lost.

According to Rabbi Kook, the second element of natural t'shuva is just being a good person.

These two components of natural t'shuva are not strictly religious concepts. They are not even exclusively Jewish. They are universal. We see them expressed in many shapes and forms — whether under the headline of physical fitness, finding oneself, discovering self-confidence, or attaining true happiness. However, it is important to note that they are all a part of the phenomenon of t'shuva.

RELIGIOUS T'SHUVA

After natural t'shuva has elevated a person by putting the person in harmony with the inner demands of his body and soul, religious t'shuva appears. This is the t'shuva which most people identify as repentance. Here, the person decides that he is not only going to be physically and morally healthy — he also longs to find favor with G-d. The directions and rules for this type of t'shuva are prescribed at length in the Torah and scholarly commentaries.[27] Here, religious tradition is needed. Without the commandments and details of Jewish law to guide him, a person would never know how to serve G-d.[28] Someone who tries to please G-d according to his own understanding and whims is serving his imagination, not G-d. He is like a fool who sneaks into a pharmacy and starts handing out capsules and pills, neither knowing the proper medicines, nor their proper amounts.[29] In the end, rather than healing people, he makes them sicker. Only by following G-d's commandments as set down in the Torah can a person hope to make a life-giving connection to G-d. For this, he needs specific directions — the tenets of Judaism.

"After the natural stage of t'shuva comes (t'shuva inspired

27. Examples are Deuteronomy, 30:2-10; *Mishne Torah, Laws of T'shuva*; *Mesillat Yesharim*; and the book *Shaare T'shuva* by Rabenu Yona Girondi.
28. *Kuzari*, by Rabbi Yehuda Halevi, 2:46.
29. *Kuzari*, 1:79.

by religious) belief. This phase of t'shuva stems from religion and tradition, which deal extensively with t'shuva. The Torah promises forgiveness for those who return from their wrongdoing. The transgressions of the individual and the community are erased through t'shuva. The prophets extol the virtues of t'shuva. In general, the entire value of the Torah's admonitions is built on t'shuva inspired by religious belief...."[30]

It is important to emphasize that Rabbi Kook sees the different phases of t'shuva as going together. Religious t'shuva is not to come at the expense of proper physical and psychological health. A person is not to be outwardly religious yet morally corrupt or physically weak. Each stage has to be based on the stage before it. First a person should be physically healthy. Then he should have a healthy state of mind. He should feel motivated to do good things and to remedy ethical shortcomings. **Once he is healthy and on a positive moral track, then he can get involved in religiosity.**[31] In doing so, he upraises his personal moral code to a higher, holier level by embracing a set of ethics which are prescribed not by the designs of his heart, but by the word of G-d as set forth in the Torah.

T'SHUVA MOTIVATED BY LOVE

Now we come to the final and most exalted stage of t'shuva. This phase also does not stand on its own, but follows after earlier stages. Once a person has a healthy body and mind,

30. *Orot HaT'shuva*, 1.
31. This is not to imply that all three levels cannot be remedied concurrently, but rather one cannot neglect other levels of t'shuva and practice religious t'shuva alone.

once he has formed an attachment to the Torah and is performing the commandments, he is ready for what Rabbi Kook calls *t'shuva sichlit*. The literal translation, intellectual t'shuva or t'shuva through reason, does not express the craving for Divine Oneness which this concept implies. This sublime phase is more closely related to t'shuva from *ahava*, from love. It is an all-encompassing return, motivated, not only by physical or spiritual wrongdoing, or by the influence of religion, whether out of fear of punishment, or through the uplifting effect of the commandments, but rather by a clear recognition which rises to expression after the natural and religious stages of t'shuva have exerted their influence — the understanding that the entire world is G-d's.

"This phase of t'shuva, which includes the earlier ones, is filled with boundless joy. It transforms all past trangressions into meritorious deeds.[32] From every act of wrongdoing it derives lofty teachings. From every humiliation, it produces glorious ascents."[33]

For example, a person who spent a lifetime lying, may decide that he wants to mend his ways. He may reach that decision because he feels an inner moral disgust. Or his decision may be formulated after learning that lying is against the laws of the Torah, and that the day of punishment awaits. However, if he gives up lying because he wants to be in harmony with the overall positive direction of existence, in line with the truth of Creation, then his t'shuva is t'shuva from love. It derives from the lofty understanding that man's highest purpose lies in

32. *Yoma* 86B.
33. *Orot HaT'shuva*, 1.

pleasing his Maker. Realizing that the entire world is being cast into imbalance by the falsehoods he utters, he seeks to mend what he has damaged. He seeks to reunite with the Universal Good. His soul longs to be at one with all of Creation. He is not motivated by a fear of punishment, nor by the desire for reward, but by a far higher inspiration — the recognition that G-d's will is directed toward absolute goodness and truth. In the illuminating light of t'shuva, he understands that the world is constantly aspiring to reach a supernal level of existence. Every minute the universe is progressing toward a redemptive, messianic ideal which he yearns to experience. He resolves to correct his wrongdoing, because he realizes that lying is antagonistic to world development and perfection. He wants to merge with the flow of life and synchronize his actions to the waves of Divine current and Divine spiritual energy which infuse all of existence. This is t'shuva out of love which is not based on anything but an absolute love and devotion to G-d. Inspired by the radiance of G-d's goodness, he determines to change all of his negative, egotistical acts into positive, transcendental ideals.

This last level of t'shuva not only atones for trangressions, but the transgressions themselves become transformed into meritorious deeds. All of the actions which brought him to this level of love, even his sins, now take on a positive light. For it was precisely his past wrongdoings which aroused his thoughts of repentance and helped him return with a purifying, burning desire to achieve oneness with G-d.

"This is the t'shuva to which everyone aspires, the t'shuva which is determined to come, and which will certainly arrive."[34]

34. *Orot HaT'shuva*, 1. For a more detailed discussion of the inevitability of t'shuva, see Chapter Six of this book.

Chapter Three

SUDDEN AND GRADUAL T'SHUVA

THE T'SHUVA TRAIN

After categorizing the different phases of t'shuva, Rabbi Kook explains how the phenomenon of t'shuva appears. T'shuva, he teaches, comes about in two distinct formats, either suddenly, or in a gradual, slowly developing fashion.

Both of these pathways to t'shuva are readily found in the *baal t'shuva* world. Some people will tell you how their lives suddenly changed overnight. Others describe their experience as a long, challenging process which unfolded over years. Many factors influence the way in which t'shuva appears, including personality, background, and environment. Health problems, whether physical or psychological, can inspire a person toward t'shuva. Personal tragedy — a death in the family, or the loss of one's job, can trigger sudden revelations of t'shuva. For others, a seemingly chance encounter with a religious Jew, a Sabbath experience, or a visit to the *Kotel* in Jerusalem has been known to set the stirrings of t'shuva in motion. Even dramatic current events, like catastrophes or wars can influence awakenings of t'shuva.

What stands out in Rabbi Kook's teaching is that the potential for t'shuva is ever-present. Like light from the sun, the waves of t'shuva constantly envelop the earth. Its spiritual force empowers mankind, silently working to bring the world back to G-d. Some people jump on the t'shuva train in one bold leap. Others climb aboard in a much slower fashion. But the train itself is always in motion.

SUDDEN T'SHUVA

Rabbi Kook writes:

"Sudden t'shuva results from a spiritual bolt of illumination which enters the soul. All at once, the person recognizes the ugliness and evil of sin, and he is transformed into a new being. Already, he feels within himself a total change for the good. This type of t'shuva derives from a certain unique inner power of the soul, from some great spiritual influence whose ways are best sought in the depths of life's mysteries."[1]

Sudden t'shuva appears when a person suddenly decides that his entire way of living needs to be changed. Revolted by the impurity of his ways, he abruptly sets out on a purer, healthier course. All at once, he feels that everything in his life must be transformed. A sudden burst of great light reveals the

1.   *Orot HaT'shuva*, 2.

sordidness of his existence, and he understands that an entire life overhaul is in order — new habits, new friends, new interests, new goals. Seemingly overnight, he is a new person. Of course, the sudden break from his old ways is not cut and dry. A person cannot change his whole existence at once. The process may take a day or a decade. But the decision which triggers this great transformation does occur in a moment of profound revelation and cleansing. A sudden, cathartic illumination lights up his being, and he is changed.

T'SHUVA IS EASY!

A discussion in the *Gemara* alludes to this type of split-second t'shuva.[2] There is a law that if a man marries a woman on the basis of some condition, the marriage is legal only if the condition is met.[3] If a man were to say, "You will be my lawfully-wedded wife on the condition that I will give you one-hundred dollars," if he gives her the money, they are married. If he does not give her the money, then the marriage does not take place.[4] What happens if a man were to marry a woman on the condition that he is a completely righteous person? Suppose that the man is a known evildoer. If he makes his righteousness the basis for the marriage, is the marriage considered proper and legal?

Jewish law states that the woman is *safek mekudeshet*,[5] married out of doubt. Yet if we know that the man is evil, how can

2.   *Kiddushin* 49B.
3.   *Shulchan Aruch, Even HaEzer*, 38:1.
4.   Ibid, Law 4.
5.   Ibid, Law 32.

this be? After all, the marriage was based on the condition that he be as righteous as a *tzaddik*. It should follow that since the condition was not kept, the woman is not married. The *Gemara* explains:

We are cautious for maybe he had a contemplation of t'shuva.[6]

We learn from this that repentance can be a split-second decision. One can become a penitent in a second, through the **thought** of t'shuva alone.

This is what Rabbi Kook is alluding to when he speaks about sudden t'shuva. Very often people are afraid to embark on a course of repentance because they believe it involves years of suffering and difficult change. Here we learn the opposite. T'shuva is easy!

The Talmud teaches that in the End of Days, G-d is going to do away with man's evil inclination.[7] Seeing this, both the righteous and evildoers react by weeping. The righteous cry when the evil inclination is shown to be as large as a mountain. The knowledge that they had to spend their lives overcoming such a formidable foe brings them to tears. The wicked cry when it is revealed to them that the evil inclination was in reality an insignificant opponent. It could have been conquered by a split-second of t'shuva, but that opportunity is now forever lost. We learn from this that the seeming darkness of sin can be swiftly erased by the great light and wonder of t'shuva.

6.   *Kiddushin* 49B.
7.   *Sukkah* 52A. Also Ramban, Deut., 30:6.

How does this type of t'shuva apply to the different stages of t'shuva which Rabbi Kook describes? In the case of natural t'shuva, a person one day decides, "That's it. I am going on a diet starting today. I want to be healthy." He strides into the kitchen and throws out all of the candies, ice creams, sodas, and chocolates. Cans of food loaded with colorings and chemical preservatives go flying into the trash. He joins a health club, moves to a place where the air is clean, and starts each new day with a jog before dawn.

Regarding the moral sphere of t'shuva, the *baal t'shuva* suddenly decides that he is fed up with the wheeling and dealing; he is weary with the struggle to get around the law; he is ashamed for the income he has failed to report; he is disgusted with his infidelities and lies. "That's it," he declares. "No more. From now on, I am going to be an honest, moral person."

From a spiritual perspective, a brilliant, sudden flash of t'shuva leaves a person disgusted with the false patterns of behavior, ideologies, and religions which he is following. As if awakening from a nightmare, he takes a deep breath, suddenly driven to align his life with the Divine truth of existence. His flash of sudden light inspires him to say, "Wow, have I been wasting my life! What a fool I have been! And I thought I was being smart! That's it. The past is forgotten. From now on, I am getting my life together with G-d!"

GRADUAL T'SHUVA

Gradual t'shuva differs from sudden t'shuva in its less dramatic, more step-by-step form. Often, when we speak about *baale t'shuva*, we are referring to people whose lives have been changed overnight. Gradual t'shuva, on the other hand, is something which often appears in a person who generally lives his life in a healthy, positive fashion. When he falls into error or sin, his recovery is more gradual, without the overwhelming illumination that comes to a person whose life has been saturated by darkness.

"There is also a gradual type of t'shuva. The change from the depths of sin to goodness is not inspired by a brilliant flash of light in one's inner self, but by the feeling that one's ways and lifestyle, one's desires, and thought processes must be improved. When a person follows this path, he gradually straightens his ways, mends his character traits, improves his deeds, and teaches himself how to correct his life more and more, until he reaches the high level of refinement and perfection."[8]

An already moral person who feels he is still far away from the goal he longs to reach, will set off on a gradual climb toward t'shuva. For him, the process of return does not revolutionize his life all at once. Rather, his perfection demands a step-by-step course of improvement. Indeed, for the average person, the best way to climb a great mountain is by taking a lot of little steps.

When this type of person goes on a diet, he does not rush into the kitchen and throw out all of the unhealthy foods all at once. Knowing that it will take time and a great deal of willpower to wean himself away from the sweets that he loves, he resolves to be fat-free within another six months. Every day, he tries to eat one donut less. He sits down and draws up a chart,

8.   *Orot HaT'shuva*, 2.

starting with one push-up and working, day-by-day, to fifty. He does not suddenly revamp his whole life. Rather, he changes it a little at a time. In this manner, he can set his life on a healthier course without dramatically altering his current comforts and habits.

Gradual t'shuva also applies in the realm of moral perfection. Character traits are not easy to alter. If one proceeds too fast by jumping to the opposite extreme, he can cause himself harm. For instance, if a greedy person decides that he has to be generous and gives all of his money to charity at once, he will not have anything left for himself. Similarly, while anger is an extremely negative trait, it is also not healthy to be unemotional and indifferent.[9] At first, a leap to the other extreme might be helpful in effecting a change, but then the penitent should gradually work his way back to the middle.[10] The Gaon of Vilna recommends that in turning a negative trait into a positive one, it is wise to set a gradual course toward reaching the middle ground between the extremes.[11] Because the change comes about slowly, a strong foundation is built. New behavior patterns formed in this fashion are likely to survive the challenges and frustrations which people face every day. In contrast, something which comes quickly, like sudden t'shuva, might, in some cases, also disappear quickly.

In regard to religious belief, gradual t'shuva also often appears when a person strives to merge his life with the Divine plan for existence. Generally, a bond and committment to religion

---

9. Rambam, Introduction to Mishna, *Avot*, Chapter Four.
10. Rambam, *Laws of De'ot*, 2:2.
11. *Even Shlema*, 1:3. See also, *Messilat Yesharim*, end of Chapter 15.

evolves slowly. After all, accepting the yoke of the Torah's commandments is not a simple matter. Not only must one's lifestyle
be altered, but the list of do's and don'ts seems overwhelming.
Of course, this is the view of the uninitiated, as seen from the
outside. Once a person steps inside the world of Judaism, what
seemed frightening in the beginning becomes a fountain of great
delight. Nonetheless, the path out of darkness to the light of the
Torah is usually a slow, step-by-step journey.

First a person comes to feel respect for the Jewish religion.
He comes to appreciate the great wisdom and beauty of Jewish
tradition. He realizes that Judaism has shaped the Jewish nation,
protected it throughout the generations, and given it its character.
But at this early stage, he is not yet ready to embrace all of the
precepts of Judaism and make them a part of his life.

Then, the more a person experiences Judaism and is stirred
by its spirit, the more he cherishes it. Feeling the great warmth
of Jewish tradition, he begins to relate to it like a long-lost
friend.

Motivated by the positive feelings which he now experiences upon each encounter with Judaism, he begins to study its
teachings in depth. His knowledge of Judaism increases. More
and more, he finds himself stimulated by the Divine genius he
discovers within it. Delving into its depths, he finds beauty and
joy in all of the commandments.

Finally, convinced of the Torah's Divine origin and truth, he
begins to practice all of its teachings.[12] He runs to perform the

12. *Orot HaT'shuva*, Ohr Etzion Edition, Appendix, Essay 8.

mitzvot with zest and enthusiasm. Nothing else in the world affords him such contentment and happiness.

The question can be asked, which of the two paths of t'shuva brings greater enlightenment — sudden or gradual. Rabbi Kook answers:

"The higher t'shuva results from a lightning-like flash of goodness, of the Divine good which dwells in all worlds, of the light of He who is the life of the worlds. The noble soul of all existence is pictured before us in all of its splendor and holiness, to the extent that the heart can absorb. Is it not true that everything is so good and upright, and that the uprightness and goodness that is within us, does it not come from our being in harmony with everything? How can we be severed from the wholeness of existence, a strange fragment, scattered into nothingness like dust? From this recognition, which is truly a Divine recognition, comes t'shuva out of love, in the life of the individual and in the life of mankind as a whole."[13]

---

13.   *Orot HaT'shuva*, 2.

Chapter Four

SPECIFIC AND GENERAL T'SHUVA

We have learned that t'shuva encompasses man's physical being, his moral life, religious life, and his highest, most ideal intellectual endeavor. T'shuva is man's path to wellbeing, to physical and emotional health, as well as his path to the deep self-discovery which connects him to G-d.

T'shuva can happen suddenly, in a burst of illumination which wonderously transforms life's darkness to light, or it can evolve over time, gradually returning the body, psyche, and soul to the true Divine path of existence.

Rabbi Kook explains that t'shuva appears in two different penitential forms: t'shuva over a specific sin or sins; and a general, all-encompassing t'shuva which completely transforms a person's whole life.

SPECIFIC T'SHUVA

If general t'shuva can be compared to a complete car over-haul, where the entire motor is removed and replaced, then specific t'shuva is like a tune-up of engine parts, a spark plug here, a cable there, new filters, oil and anti-freeze.

Specific t'shuva is commonly referred to as penitence. It is the t'shuva familiar to everyone, whereby a person sins, feels guilty, and decides to redress his wrongdoing. Rabbi Kook believes in the basic goodness of man. In his natural, moral, pristine state, man is a happy, healthy creature. When a man sins, his natural state is altered, and the difference causes him pain. Sin causes a distortion. It creates a barrier between man and his natural pure essence and source. Most essentially, sin damages man's connection to G-d. The feeling which results, whether we call it anxiety, pain, darkness, guilt, or remorse, impels the sinner to correct his wrongdoing, in order to return to the proper course of living. The sorrow which stems from transgression acts as an atonement, and the sinner is cleansed. Returned to his original state of wellbeing, the melancholy and darkness of sin is replaced by the joy and light of the renewed connection to goodness and G-d.

"There is a type of t'shuva which focuses on a specific sin, or many specific sins. The individual confronts his wrongdoing directly, regrets it, and feels sorry that he was ensnared in the trap of transgression. Then his soul climbs and ascends until he is freed from sinful bondage. He feels in his midst a holy freedom which brings comfort to his weary soul. His healing proceeds; the glimmers of light of a merciful sun, shining with Divine forgiveness, send him their rays, and, together with his broken heart and feelings of depression, a feeling of inner happiness graces his life...."[1]

There are times in everyone's life when a person decides to change a particular habit, to improve a trait, or to right some outstanding wrong. He is not looking to change his whole life. Generally he is content, but he senses a need to remedy a specific failing. If a person realizes that he is stingy, he may decide that he wants to be more charitable. Or he may feel a pressing need to return a tennis racket which he stole. In the same light, a religious person may realize that his prayers lack enthusiasm and proper concentration. So he sets out to pray with more fervor. In these cases his t'shuva deals with a specific life problem which he sets out to correct.

THE HEALING POWER OF REMORSE

A person whose soul is sensitive to moral wrongdoing will feel remorse for his sins. The remorse weighs down on him, and he longs to break free from its shackles. The longing to redress his wrongdoing works like a force to shatter the darkness, opening a window of light. This light of t'shuva is a stream of Divine mercy. It is as if G-d reaches out and accepts the repenter's remorse. The sin is forgiven. The path back to G-d has been cleared. Instead of darkness and gloom, happiness envelops the soul.

"He experiences this (happiness) at the same time that his heart remains shattered, and his spirit feels lowly and sad. In fact, this melancholy feeling suits him in his situation, adding to

1.   *Orot HaT'shuva*, 3.

his inner spiritual gladness and his sense of true wholeness. He feels himself coming closer to the Source of life, to the living G-d, who had been so distant from him a short time before. His longing spirit jubilantly remembers its former inner pain, and, filled with emotions of gratitude, it raises its voice in song and praise:

"Bless the L-rd, O my soul, and do not forget all of His goodness; He forgives all thy iniquities, heals all thy diseases; redeems thy life from the pit; adorns thee with love and compassion; and satiates thy old age with good, so that thy youth is renewed like the eagle's. The L-rd performs righteousness and judgment for all who are oppressed."[2]

The person who sins and feels remorse senses its cleansing power. He recognizes his pain as an atonement, and this brings him relief. Almost miraculously, the clouds of his transgression are lifted, and the light of t'shuva fills his being with joy. He senses that it is G-d who has freed him, and his heart abounds with gratitude and song.

In describing the inner workings of t'shuva, Rabbi Kook does not enumerate the halachic laws of repentance which can be found in other books. For instance, the Rambam's *Laws of T'shuva* sets forth the steps a person must take in redressing transgression.[3] Among the many details, a penitent must confess his sin, feel remorse, abandon his wrongdoing, amend his ways, and never commit the transgression again.[4] Rabbi Kook presumes that

---

2. Psalms, 103:2-6. *Orot HaT'shuva*, 3.
3. Rambam, *Laws of T'shuva*, Chapter 2.
4. Ibid, 2:2.

his reader has a knowledge of these laws. His purpose, as made clear in his introduction, is to illuminate the overall phenomenon and importance of t'shuva in the life of the individual, the Jewish nation, and the world.

Summing up his analysis of specific t'shuva, Rabbi Kook describes a journey from darkness to light:

"How downtrodden was the soul when the burden of sin, its darkness, vulgarity, and horrible suffering lay upon it. How lowly and oppressed the soul was, even if external riches and honor fell in its portion. What good is there in wealth if life's inner substance is poor and stale? How joyful the soul is now with the inner conviction that its iniquity has been forgiven, that G-d's nearness is living and glowing inside it, that its inner burden has been lightened, that its debt (of atonement) has already been paid, and that it is no longer anguished by inner turmoil and oppression. The soul is filled with rest and rightful tranquility. *Return to thy rest, O my soul, for the L-rd has dealt bountifully with thee.*"[5]

PSYCHIATRY OR T'SHUVA

Interestingly, the process of anguish, depression, catharsis, and joy which Rabbi Kook describes parallels the psychiatric journey, or the quest for happiness in our time. Vast numbers of people are depressed and unhappy. The world's pleasures can only bring them a few fleeting moments of delight. Their lives are plagued by darkness, anxiety, and inner despair. Modern psychiatry, and all of the popular books on the subject, offer a gamut

5.   Psalms, 116:7. *Orot HaT'shuva*, 3.

of explanations, solutions, treatments, and cures. They too promise catharthis and joy. But all too often, after some initial relief, the patient is back on the couch, or back in the bookstore searching for the newest bestseller.

In Rabbi Kook's explanation of specific t'shuva and general t'shuva what strikes us is his understanding of human psychology. **While psychiatrists offer many theories about man's existential dilemma and angst, Rabbi Kook reveals that the real cause of humanity's malaise stems from mankind's severance from G-d.** The solution, he teaches, is t'shuva.

GENERAL T'SHUVA

As we study Rabbi Kook's explanation of general t'shuva, how remarkably it sounds like a description of the anxiety and spiritual darkness of our age:

"There is another type of feeling of t'shuva — a vague, general t'shuva. Past sin or sins do not weigh on a person's heart. Rather he has a general feeling of profound inner depression, that he is filled with sin, that G-d's light does not shine on him, that there is nothing noble in his being. He senses that his heart is sealed, and that his personality and traits are not on the straight and desirable path that is worthy of gracing a pure soul with a wholesome life. He feels that his intellectual insights are primitive, and that his emotions are mixed with darkness and lusts which awake within him a spiritual repulsion. He is ashamed of himself; he knows that G-d is not within him; and this is his greatest anguish, his most frightening sin. He is embittered with himself; he can find no escape from his snare which involves no specific wrongdoing, rather it is as if his entire being is imprisoned in dungeon locks.

"From out of this psychic bitterness, t'shuva comes as a healing plaster from an expert physician. The feeling of t'shuva — with a deep insight into its working and its deep foundation in the recesses of the soul, in the hidden realms of nature, in all the chambers of Torah, faith and tradition — with all of its power, comes and streams into his soul. A mighty confidence in its healing, the encompassing rebirth which t'shuva affords to all who cling to it, surrounds the person with a spirit of grace and mercy. *Like a man is comforted by his mother, so I shall comfort you.*"[6]

This description of depression, darkness, inner shame and despair is an exact description of modern man's psychic condition. Whether it is termed psychological neurosis by Sigmund Freud, primal angst by Carl Jung, anxiety by Rollo May, or feeling not-OK by Thomas Harris, the symptoms are the same.

Thus, when Joe Cohen walks gloomily into a bookstore looking for a paperback bestseller on how to be happy, he should also look for a Rabbi Kook book on t'shuva. Instead of phoning a shrink, he should have a good, long talk with a rabbi.

In emphasizing that t'shuva is the cure for mankind's anxiety and depression, we do not intend to negate the contributions of psychology and its related fields. Psychology has its place. For instance, an insecure youth will experience a feeling of liberation when he realizes that his parents are smothering him.

6.   Isaiah, 66:13. *Orot HaT'shuva*, 3.

The feelings of repressed anger which were causing him depression now can be dealt with. Similarly, when a man in couples-therapy realizes that he feels in competition with his wife because of unresolved childhood hang-ups with his brother, he will feel liberated to embark on a healthier marriage. However, while childhood traumas influence behavior and cause great confusion and pain, when they are finally uncovered and resolved, the catharsis which results is only a step along the way. Until an individual erases all of the "neuroses" or barriers which separate him from G-d, he will remain estranged from his self, imprisoned in darkness, living either like an unfeeling zombie, or in depression and pain. Psychology and its branches can give him a start, but ultimately, the only real cure is t'shuva.[7]

A NEW BEING

Rabbi Kook explains just how the healing takes place:

"With each passing day, powered by this lofty general t'shuva, his feeling becomes more secure, clearer, more enightened with the light of intellect, and more clarified according to the foundations of Torah. His demeanor becomes brighter,

---

7. It must also be noted that while psychiatry has its place, psychiatric theory can be severely misleading. For instance, Freud, in his book, *Totem and Taboo*, maintained that religion was a product of man's primitive fears (the totem theory) whereby man invents controlling forces to worship to protect him against nature and the unknown. Rabbi Kook, however, sees that man's basic fear is the fear of sin, which is a healthy and positive attribute which should be encouraged, not denigrated or repressed. *Orot HaT'shuva*, 6:3.

his anger subsides, the light of grace shines on him. He becomes filled with strength; his eyes are filled with a holy fire; his heart is completely immersed in springs of pleasure; holiness and purity envelop him. A boundless loves fills all of his spirit; his soul thirsts for G-d, and this very thirst satiates all of his being. The holy spirit rings before him like a bell, and he is informed that all of his willful transgressions, the known and the unknown, have been erased; that he has been reborn as a new being; that all of the world and all of Creation are reborn with him; that all of existence calls out in song, and that the joy of G-d infuses all. *Great is t'shuva for it brings healing to the world,*[8] and *even one individual who repents is forgiven and the whole world is forgiven with him.*"[9]

General overall t'shuva does not come to mend anything specific. It occurs when a person feels lost, surrounded by darkness, cut off from G-d. In this drastic state, a total revamping is needed. The rotted foundations of this person's lifestyle must be uprooted, and a new Divine foundation be built in its place. But where does one start? First by longing. By longing for G-d. This leads to prayer, a calling out for G-d from the darkness. Indeed, the search for a holier life will bring a person to discover two life-saving essentials of t'shuva — prayer and Torah. Prayer is man's ladder to G-d.[10] By expressing man's longing for his Maker, prayer builds a bridge between the physical world

8.   *Yoma* 86A. *Orot HaT'shuva*, 3.
9.   *Yoma* 86B.
10. "Prayers and supplications to G-d, and t'shuva from the depths of the heart, which is actively realized in the mending of one's ways, must precede every appearance of the light of higher perception." *Orot HaT'shuva*, 10:11.

and the spiritual world. Once a connection has been made, man can begin to hear the "voice" of G-d calling back. G-d communicates with man through the Torah. It is G-d's will for the world, His plan for our lives. Discovering Torah, man discovers true light. Finally, he knows what to do. He knows how to act. With the guidelines of Torah, he learns to distinguish between good and evil, between pure and impure. In the past, his life was guided by his own ethical sense and desires, without ever knowing what was absolutely moral and just. Suddenly the darkness and uncertainty are gone. Anxiety vanishes. In the light of the Torah, his soul finds instant rest, secure that it has found the right path. Once again united with the Divine song of existence, he brings himself, and the whole world, closer to G-d.

Chapter Five

T'SHUVA MAKES THE WORLD GO ROUND

BEFORE THE WORLD WAS CREATED

The *Gemara* teaches that t'shuva existed before the world was created.[1] In a similar vein, Rabbi Kook writes that the spirit of t'shuva hovers over the world and gives it its basic form and the motivation to develop. It is t'shuva which gives the world its direction and its inner energy to constantly progress. The desire to refine the world and to embellish it with beauty and splendor all derive from the spirit of t'shuva.[2]

T'shuva is the Divine, spiritual force in the universe which is constantly propelling all of existence toward perfection. It is

1. *Pesachim* 54A. Also *Orot HaT'shuva,* 5:6a.
2. *Orot HaT'shuva,* 5:4.

the voice of G-d calling, *Return to Me, you children of men.*[3] Due to the "separation" from G-d through transgressions, improper living, or through the act of Creation itself, there is a constant drive in all things to return to a harmony with their Maker. Rabbi Kook writes that, "It is impossible to express this awesomely deep idea."[4] **The force of t'shuva, like gravity in the physical world, is built into the inner fabric of life. It stands as the impetus behind all human history, all world development, all endeavor toward social improvement.** It is the force which inspires all cultural, artistic, and scientific advancement. Similarly, the yearning of mankind for universal justice and moral perfection is a product of the encompassing, ever-present power of t'shuva.

On a personal level, when a man sells his house in the country because he wants to improve the quality of his life, he is involved in t'shuva. When a family has a fun and relaxing vacation, they are being motivated by forces of t'shuva. Though there may be underlying factors of profit and self-interest when a pharmaceutical company produces a new drug, they too are involved in t'shuva, if their product truly helps to benefit the world.[5]

"T'shuva derives from the yearning of all existence to be better, purer, more fortified and elevated than it is. Hidden within this desire is a life-force capable of overcoming that which limits and weakens existence. The personal t'shuva of an individual, and even more so of the community, draws its

3.   Psalms, 90:3.
4.   *Orot HaT'shuva*, 4:1.
5.   See *Michtav M'Eliyahu*, by Rabbi Eliyahu Dessler, Volume One, pg. 270.

strength from this source of life which is constantly active with never-ending vigor."[6]

NEVER-ENDING T'SHUVA

In his writings, Rabbi Kook illuminates the phenomenon of t'shuva in an entirely new fashion. Here we encounter the notion of t'shuva, not as personal penitence alone, but as an ever-active force in the world which constantly works to unite all things with G-d.

"The currents of specific and general t'shuva[7] flood along. They resemble waves of flames on the surface of the sun, which break free and ascend in a never-ending struggle, granting life to numerous worlds and numberless creatures. It is impossible to grasp the multitude of colors of this great sun that lights all worlds, the sun of t'shuva, because of their abundance and wonderous speed, because they emanate from the Source of life itself...."[8]

In his poetic style, Rabbi Kook describes t'shuva like a sun which sends out constant flames of warming light to the world. Just as G-d has created the sun as life's principle energy source, so too is t'shuva the spiritual energy source of existence. **T'shuva does not only operate when a person decides to mend his erring ways; t'shuva exists all of the time.** It exists both within man and all around him, as a personal t'shuva, and as

6. *Orot HaT'shuva*, 6:1.
7. For an explanation of specific and general t'shuva, see Chapter Five of this book.
8. *Orot HaT'shuva*, 4:1.

a t'shuva which comes from Above. Like gravity, or the wind, or the rays of the sun, t'shuva is ever present. It is a constant force always at work, bringing the world to completion. One day the force may hit Jonathan; the next day Miriam; one day soon it will uplift the Jewish people as a whole. Its waves flow by us in a continuous stream. Minute by minute, the song of t'shuva calls out to us to hurry and join in the flow.

UNION WITH G-D

Now that we recognize that t'shuva is an independent force which G-d has implanted into the fabric of Creation, we must ask, what does it do?

Throughout his writings on t'shuva, Rabbi Kook has to clothe his profound understandings in a wardrobe of metaphors to express the workings of t'shuva.

"The individual and the collective soul, the world soul, the soul of all worlds of Creation, roars like a mighty lioness in agony for complete perfection, for the ideal existence; and we experience the pain, and it purges us like salt sweetens meat, the pain sweetens our bitterness."[9]

Rabbi Kook emphasizes that the soul grows toward perfection.[10] The soul has a built-in motor that guides it toward perfection. The perfection it seeks is the union with G-d. This is what King David is expressing when he says, *Of Thee my heart*

9.   Ibid.
10.   Ibid.

has said, 'Seek My Presence.' Thy Presence, Hashem, I will seek.[11] One unites with G-d when one has a knowledge of G-d and performs His will. G-d's will is housed in this world in the Torah and its commandments.

What empowers the soul to seek out its Maker? What gives it fuel for the quest? The power of t'shuva.

"Through the force of t'shuva all things return to G-d. By the existence of t'shuva's power which prevails in all worlds, all things are returned and reconnected to the realm of Divine perfection. Through concepts of t'shuva, understandings of t'shuva, and feelings of t'shuva, all thoughts, ideas, understandings, desires, and emotions are transformed and return to their essential character in line with Divine holiness."[12]

Before continuing, it may be beneficial to say a few words about the concept of returning to G-d. What does this mean? Where have we gone that we need to return? This is a very profound question, and only the beginnings of an answer will be given here. The soul, in its essence, belongs to the world of souls. When it is placed in this world, in a physical body, it naturally longs to go home.[13] For the soul, going home is being reunited with G-d.[14] One of the great innovations of Judaism is the teaching that this reunion is not limited to the return of the soul to "Heaven" after the death of the body. **Unlike other religions, Judaism teaches that the soul can find union with G-d**

11.   Psalms, 27:8.
12.   *Orot HaT'shuva*, 4:2.
13.   Maharal, *Netiv HaT'shuva*, Chapter 2.
14.   Ibid.

in this world.[15] This union is brought about when a Jew performs the Torah's commandments.

The expulsion of Adam and Eve from the Garden of Eden describes man's existential plight. In effect, the sum of world history is mankind's journey to return to the Garden. Not only man, but the world itself wants to return to its original state.[16] This yearning is one of the most powerful forces of Creation. Thus the world "roars like a mighty lioness"[17] to return to its original, ideal closeness to G-d.[18]

WORLD REDEMPTION

Once we understand that the goal of existence is to be re-united with G-d, and that the force of t'shuva is at work all of the time, we can understand that the t'shuva of the individual over specific sins, and the encompassing t'shuva of the world longing for perfection, all stem from the same essential drive.

"General t'shuva, which is the uplifting of the world to perfection; and specific t'shuva, which relates to the particular personality of each individual, including the smallest items needing improvement in all of their details... they are both of one essence. So too, all of the cultural reforms which lift the world out

15. *Kuzari*, 3:11.
16. *Yalkut Shimoni, Bechukotai, 672.* Also, *Orot HaT'shuva*, 6:7.
17. *Orot HaT'shuva*, 4:2.
18. For a more in-depth, Kabbalistic explanation of this matter, see Rabbi Yaacov Filber's *Commentary on Orot HaT'shuva*, Chapter 4, Footnote 8, pg. 29, published by the Research Institute for the Writings of Rabbi Avraham Yitzhak HaCohen Kook, Jerusalem, Fourth Edition, 5757.

of moral decay, along with social and economic advancements, and the mending of all transgression... all of them comprise a single entity, and are not detached one from the other."[19]

The perfection of all of the different people and ideologies in the world really represents one giant unified t'shuva. To understand this deep idea, it may help to momentarily substitute another word for t'shuva when we speak about the t'shuva of culture, society, and ultimately of the world. Instead of the word t'shuva, let's use the word *geula*, or redemption. To Rabbi Kook, t'shuva and redemption share the same direction and goal — to bring healing to a suffering world. Redemption is the ever-active historical process which brings the nation of Israel and the world to perfection and completion. The zenith of redemption is reached at the End of Days with the arrival of *Mashiach* and Israel's great material and spiritual rennaisance. When this great day arrives, the Kingdom of G-d will be established throughout the world; Israel will be recognized as His truly chosen people; the nations will flock to Jerusalem to learn the laws of the G-d of Jacob; and truth and justice will reign supreme.[20] In this glorious future, prophecy will be reestablished in Israel, and life itself will experience the zenith of t'shuva when the dead are resurrected from their graves.[21]

Using the concept of redemption to illuminate our understanding of world perfection, we can better appreciate Rabbi Kook's great vision of t'shuva.

---

19.   *Orot HaT'shuva*, 4:3.
20.   Isaiah, 2:3.
21.   Ibid, 26:19. See the commentaries of the Radak and the Malbim there.

"With each second, in the depths of life, a new illumination of supreme t'shuva shines ever forth, just as a new glowing light constantly sparkles through all realms of existence and replenishes them.... The fruit of the highest forms of moral and practical culture, blossom and grow in the flow of this light. In truth, the light of the whole world and its renewal in all of its forms, in every time and age, depends on t'shuva. This is especially true regarding the light of *Mashiach*, the salvation of Israel, the rebirth of the Jewish nation and its Land, language, and literature — all of them stem from the source of t'shuva, and all will emerge from the depths to the exalted reaches of the highest t'shuva."[22]

T'shuva and redemption are parallel processes, reaching the same destination. The main difference between them is one of style and not of substance. For example, redemption has a broad historical, international base with political consequences. Though there are differences between them, these two phenomona are closely intertwined, so that when Rabbi Kook speaks about the t'shuva of the entire world, he is speaking about its overall moral, material, and spiritual redemption.[23]

THE ENCOMPASSING PERSPECTIVE

As we learned, mankind is always involved in t'shuva. The fact that there are many non-religious people today should not

---

22. *Orot HaT'shuva*, 4:11.
23. See Chapter Sixteen of this book for an in-depth discussion on the connection between the redemption of Israel and the redemption of the world.

be held up as a contradiction. T'shuva must be looked at in an undivided perspective that spans all generations.

A story about Rabbi Kook may help illustrate this. One day, Rabbi Kook was walking by the Old City in Jerusalem with Rabbi Chaim Zonnenfeld, one of the leading rabbis of the Orthodox community.

"Look how awful our situation is," the rabbi observed. "See how many secular Jews there our in the city. Just a few generations ago, their father's fathers were all Orthodox Jews."

"One must look at *Am Yisrael* in a wider perspective," Rabbi Kook answered. "Do you see this valley over here, the Valley of Hinom? This was once a site for human sacrifice. Today, even the crassest secularist will not offer his child as a human sacrifice for any pagan ideal. When you look at today's situation in the span of all history, things do not seem so bad. On the contrary, you can see that there has been great progress."

CHRISTIANITY AS A STEPPING STONE

The Rambam, at the end of the Laws of Kings,[24] refers to this same development process of redemption which encompasses all things in life. He asks the question — if Christianity is a false religion, why did G-d grant it so much dominion? In the time of the Rambam, Christianity and Islam ruled over the world. The Jews suffered miserably under both. The Rambam's answer is based on a sweeping historical perspective which finds

---

24.   Rambam, *Laws of Kings*, 11:4, in the uncensored Frankel edition.

a certain value in Christianity even though the Rambam himself classifies Christianity as idol worship.[25] On the one hand, he unequivically condemns Christianity, and on the other hand he maintains that Christianity has a positive role in the development of world history. How are we to reconcile this contradiction?

The Rambam writes that Christianity serves as a facilitator to elevate mankind from the darkness of paganism toward the recognition of monotheism. In effect, it is a stepping stone enabling mankind to make the leap from idol worship to the worship of G-d. The belief in an invisible G-d does not come easily to the masses. Christianity, weaned mankind away from the belief in many gods to a belief in a triumverate of a father, a son, and a holy ghost.[26] Once the world is accustomed to this idea, though it is still idol worship, the concept of one supreme G-d is not so removed. Furthermore, the Rambam writes that Christianity's focus on the messiah prepares the world for the day when the true Jewish messiah will come. Today, because of Christianity's influence, all of the world, from Eskimos to Zulus, have heard about the messiah, so that when he arrives, he will have a lot less explaining to do. "Oh, it's you," mankind will say on the heralded day. "We've been waiting for you."

Thus, when world history is looked at in an encompassing perspective, even Christianity, with all of its many negative fac-

---

25. Rambam, *Laws of Idol Worship*, 9:4, in the uncensored Rabbi Kapach edition.

26. *Kuzari*, 4:23. See the *Otzar Nechmad* commentary there.

tors,[27] can be seen to play a positive role in mankind's constant march toward t'shuva.

THE UNITY OF CREATION

When we understand this historic, all-encompassing perspective, we can see that a world movement like Christianity, despite all of its evil, can influence the course of human history toward a higher ideal. But how does one man's t'shuva bring redemption closer? How does a person's remorse over having stolen some money bring healing to the cosmos as a whole?

The answer is that one is to look on each individual, not as a unit separated from the rest of the world, but as being integrally united with all of Creation.

"The nature of the world and of every individual creature, the entire sweep of human history and the life of every person, and his deeds, must be viewed from one all-encompassing perspective, as one unity made up of many parts...."[28]

A man is not a fragmented being disconnected from the past and the future. He is part of the continuity of generations. He is a part of his national history and a sweeping world drama. In the same way that he is a product of his past, he is also the

27. For Rabbi Kook's writings on the pernicious influences of Christianity, see the book, *War and Peace*, Chapters Five and Eight, Rabbi David Samson and Tzvi Fishman, Torat Eretz Yisrael Publications. Also *Orot, Yisrael U'Techiyato,* Rabbi Kook, pgs. 20-34, Mosad HaRav Kook Publishers. Also, *Tzemach Tzvi,* Letters of Rabbi Tzvi Yehudah Kook, Letter 71.

28. *Orot HaT'shuva,* 4:4.

seed of the future. When a man sees himself in this wider per-spective, the t'shuva he does for personal sins is magnified by his connection to all generations. Thus, his personal t'shuva is up-lifted by the general t'shuva of the world, which strengthens his own drive to do good. This merging of an individual's t'shuva with the mighty stream of the universal will for goodness is the source of the great joy which t'shuva always brings.

"T'shuva comes forth from the profoundest depths, from the vast depths where the individual is not a separate entity, but rather a continuation of the greatness which pervades uni-versal existence. The yearning for t'shuva (on a personal level) is connected to the world's yearning for t'shuva at its most ex-alted source. And since the great current of the flow of life's yearning is directed toward doing good, immediately many streams flow through all of existence to reveal goodness and to bring benefit to all."[29]

For example, as a wheel axis spins, the spokes and the whole wheel spins with it. So too, a person who steals should not look at his theft as his own personal dilemma, he should see his stealing as something that damages the moral environ-ment around him, and this adds evil to the society where he lives, and this increases the evil in the world. When he starts re-turning the money he took, he adds goodness to the world and

---

29. *Orot HaT'shuva*, 6:1. For a detailed discussion on how man's good actions and thoughts in the lower world give strength to the powers of goodness in the higher realms, and how they, in turn, increase the forces of goodness below, see *Nefesh HaChaim*, Gate One, Chapters Four and Five, by Rabbi Chaim of Volozin. See also, *Orot HaT'shuva*, 6:6.

brings all of existence closer to moral perfection. Like a stone thrown into a pool, his individual t'shuva sends waves of t'shuva rippling through all realms of life, from his family and immediate surroundings, to his community, his nation, and the world. Because his soul is attached to the soul of the world, in purifying his soul, he helps purify all realms of being.[30]

Thus, Rabbi Kook writes that it is impossible to quantify the importance of practical t'shuva, the correcting of one's behavior in accordance with the Torah, which raises the soul of the individual and the soul of the community to higher and higher levels. Every step along the way contains myriads of ideals and horizons of light.[31]

This understanding led our Sages to say that *Great is t'shuva, for it brings healing to the world,*[32] and *even one individual who repents is forgiven and the whole world is forgiven with him.*[33]

"The more we contemplate to what extent the smallest details of existence, the spiritual and the material, are microcosms containing the general principles, and understand that every

---

30. Rabbi Kook writes, "An individual's existence is connected to universal existence by a very strong bond, and when a part of existence is elevated, all of existence is automatically lifted up with it. In this way, every good deed truly improves countless worlds. When a person embraces this understanding, his mind is expanded and his contemplations come closer and closer to the truth." *Musar Avicha, Midot, Tikun,* 1.

31. *Orot HaT'shuva,* 12:6.

32. *Yoma* 86A.

33. Ibid, 86B. *Orot HaT'shuva,* 6:1.

small detail bears imprints of greatness in the depths of its be-ing[34] — we will no longer wonder about the secret of t'shuva which so deeply penetrates man's soul, encompassing him from the beginning of his thoughts and beliefs to the most exacting details of his deeds and character.... When we will know more about the qualitative value of man and his spirit, and about the character which his imprint gives to existence, we will imme-diately perceive the glowing relationship between the great cos-mic t'shuva, in all of its breadth, depth, and loftiness, and the t'shuva of man, the individual and the community, around which all of the stratagems of practical and spiritual life re-volve."[35]

When a man understands that his personal t'shuva ad-vances the redemptional process of the world, his motivation to mend his own life is enhanced. His own personal t'shuva ex-pands beyond his life's limited boundaries and brings benefit to all of mankind. No longer dwelling on escaping his own per-sonal darkness, he altruistically yearns to bring greater illumi-nation to the world. This is the zenith of t'shuva.

34. Kabbalistic terminology describes man as being a small world. See Ramak's commentary to *Sefer HaYetzira* 3:4. See also, *Duties of the Heart, Shaar HaBechina*, Ch. 5, by Rabbi Bachya Ibn Paquda, "When we have arrived at an understanding of the matters noted in regard to man, much of the mystery of this universe will become clear to us, since the one resembles the other."

35. *Orot HaT'shuva*, 11:4.

Chapter Six

DEATH, TAXES, AND T'SHUVA

T'SHUVA MUST COME

There is an old aphorism which claims that two things in life are certain: death and taxes. To this, Rabbi Kook would add a third certainty — t'shuva. Before we begin to explore the multi-faceted world of t'shuva, as it applies to the individual and to existence as a whole, it is important to know that the return to the Source is inevitable. Just as the body has a built-in mechanism for self-healing, so does mankind. T'shuva is promised, and t'shuva will come. The world will return to its Maker.

"The world must come to a state of complete t'shuva. The world is not static; rather it progresses and develops, and the true, complete development must inevitably bring absolute health, both physical and spiritual, and this will bring the light of the life of t'shuva with it."[1]

1. *Orot HaT'shuva*, 5:3.

Webster's Dictionary defines determinism as: "a doctrine which postulates that acts of the will, occurrences in nature, or social or psychological phenomena are determined by antecedent causes." In Rabbi Kook's era, the theory of determinism was the talk of the town. Darwin theorized that the world was deterministically guided by a course of evolution. Marx declared that communism was deterministic in nature. The Americans claimed that capitalism, not communism, was destined to conquer the world. Zionists said that the Jewish people were deterministically driven to have their own state. Freud insisted that man was deterministically motivated by the events of his past.

As if observing the world from the top of a mountain peak, Rabbi Kook wrote that behind all of these social, political, and scientific movements was the movement of movements, the determinism of determinisms — t'shuva. At the root of them all, the inner force of t'shuva was constantly pushing the world forward to make it a better place. When the t'shuva force hits a political thinker like Marx, the Communist Manifesto is born. When it hits Herzl, it results in a book, *The Jewish State*. When it hits a deep, spiritual thinker like Rabbi Kook, it becomes *Orot HaT'shuva*. T'shuva can take many forms, depending on the person, and the extent to which he has purified himself. However, one thing is common to all, whether it be the drive to build a utopian society; to abolish poverty and disease; to prevent aging and death; to produce healthier foods; to ban nucleur weapons; to protect the environment; and to guarantee equal rights for all minority groups — all of these things are driven by t'shuva.

WORLD DEVELOPMENT

The comforting words of Rabbi Kook as he passed by the Valley of Hinom in Jerusalem[2] come to assure us that the world is indeed becoming a better place. After all, people no longer sacrifice their children to the gods. There is a deterministic trend in the world toward improvement and progress. While parts of mankind are still gripped by primitive superstitions and customs, world civilization has come a long way since the days of Ghengis Khan. The Dark Ages gave way to the Renaissance with its focus on art and literature. With the Age of Enlightenment and the Industrial Revolution, mankind took another leap forward. Where once man lived in fear of forces he could not control, now he felt that his intelligence and reason could lead him to master the world. In modern times, the Fall of the Bastille and the Age of Emancipation, have brought great benefit to mankind. Generally, the world is a healthier place than it was just a few decades ago. This world development is all a part of t'shuva.

As we mentioned in Chapter One, not only is mankind destined for t'shuva, the animal world, the plant world, even the sun and the moon are all destined to return to their original purity. Our Sages teach that one day the lion will lie down with the lamb;[3] the taste of a tree's bark will be the same as its fruit;[4] and the moon will be as large as the sun.[5]

---

2. Chapter Five, pg. 59.
3. Rambam, *Laws of Kings*, 12:1. Isaiah, 11:6.
4. *Yalkut Shimoni, Bechukotai, 672.*
5. Isaiah, 30:26. *Shmot Rabbah,* 18:11.

NOTHING IS MORE CERTAIN

One might argue that while the world constantly develops in cultural and material spheres, spiritual t'shuva is destined to remain a dream. Individuals, yes, there are always a few oddballs that latch onto religion, but the world? "In G-d we trust" may be written on the dollar, but the dollar is worshipped far more. Not only that, but violence and murder are rampant all over the world. And in the matter of sexual purity, man today is not much more elevated than the average Viking of the past. Nonetheless, Rabbi Kook has hope.

"T'shuva is ever-present in the heart. Even at the moment of transgression itself, t'shuva is hidden in the soul, and it sends out it's rays which afterward are revealed when remorse calls out for t'shuva. In the depths of life, t'shuva exists, since t'shuva preceded the world, and before sin occurred, the remedy of t'shuva had already been prepared. Therefore, nothing is more certain in the world than t'shuva, and in the end, everything will return to its perfected state."[6]

Rabbi Kook continues by saying that the certainty of t'shuva is all the more guaranteed regarding the nation of Israel, whose t'shuva is promised.[7] Israel stands waiting to return to its original holy yearning for G-d, to express in life the true nature of its soul, in every facet of its nationhood and being,

---

6.   *Orot HaT'shuva*, 6:2.
7.   Ibid. Deut., 30:2-6. Ezekiel, 36:24-28. *Sanhedrin* 97B-98A. See also, Rambam, *Laws of T'shuva*, 7:8.

"in spite of all the iron curtains which are blocking the manifestation of this mighty inner essence."[8]

In upcoming chapters,[9] we will learn more about the t'shuva of the Jewish people. The true nature of Israel's soul is *kedusha*, or holiness.[10] Our Sages tell us that Israel and Torah are one, sharing the same Divine source.[11] While this holiness exists at the core of every Jewish soul, as its inheritance from our holy forefathers, it is the task of every Jew to make holiness the guiding force of his life. If a Jew ignores this aspect of his being, he simply will not feel it. He won't even know it exists. If he does not develop this most intrinsic part of himself, he will come to identify with the norms of the culture around him. This is like the story of the boy who was raised by wolves in a forest — he thought that he too was a wolf. But this, Rabbi Kook assures us, is just a passing phase of our history which will one day lead us back to our roots.

"The abandonment and rebellion against the commandments of G-d is a terrible moral regression, which only seizes a man through his frightening immersion in the vulgarness of material life. It is possible that for a time, a generation, or a part of it, in one place or another, will become entagled in the thicket of moral blindness, to the point that it won't sense at all the ethical descent inherent in the abandonment of the laws of G-d. But the Divine law does not lose its value because of this. T'shuva is determined to come and to be revealed. For the

8. *Orot HaT'shuva*, 6:2.
9. Chapters 17-20.
10. Letters of Rabbi Kook, Letter 555, Mosad HaRav Kook Publishers.
11. *Zohar, Vayikra*, 73A-B.

sickness of forgetting the Divine world cannot hold a permanent place in man's nature. Like a polluted spring, it returns to its purity."[12]

T'SHUVA FEVER

Since t'shuva is inevitable, it behooves us to get on the proverbial boat. After all, who wants to lose out on a good thing? Once we know that t'shuva is the real goal in life, why waste time on pursuing illusory things like money, power, and fame? Simply because they don't seem so illusory. Today, the world is dominated by materialism. In truth, the great leaps forward in technology and science are all leading life toward greater capabilities, but all too often, people get caught up in the race to achieve, to succeed, to consume, to enjoy, and thus they lose sight of loftier goals. In a competitive, capitalistic culture, people tend to live for "me" and not for "us." Things like morality in big business, and in our private lives, can easily be overlooked. While all over the globe, one can find seekers ardently trying to "return to their roots," the t'shuva movement still does not attract as many people as Disney. But this, Rabbi Kook, insists is destined to change.

"The future will reveal the miracle of the power of t'shuva, and this revelation will capture the whole world with an incredible fervor, far greater than all of the wonders which the world is accustomed to see in all of the realms of life and existence. And this new revelation will captivate every heart with its wonder, and its spirit will influence all people. Then the world will rise to its true rebirth. Sin will cease, the spirit of

---

12. *Orot HaT'shuva*, 6:4.

impurity will be consumed as if burned, and evil will vanish like smoke."[13]

One day the world is going to get "turned on" to t'shuva.[14] T'shuva is going to be the final world craze. Everyone will want to do it. No other fad will come after it. Nothing will ever take its place.

13. *Orot HaT'shuva,* 5:7.

14. Zacharia, 8:22-23, "And many peoples and mighty nations shall come to seek the L-rd of Hosts in Jerusalem... and they shall take hold of the corners of the garment of a Jew, saying, 'Let us go with you for we have heard that G-d is with you.'"

Chapter Seven

THE JOY OF T'SHUVA

THE WORLD'S GREATEST JOY

Jews who have become religious, *baale t'shuva*, describe t'shuva as the most joyous experience in their lives. Very often, a gleam of happiness shines in their eyes. Their speech is filled with an excited ring, as if they have discovered a secret treasure. Even people who have tasted all of life's secular pleasures insist that the experience of t'shuva is the world's greatest joy.

What is the reason for this? What is the source of this joy?

"T'shuva is the healthiest feeling possible. A healthy soul in a healthy body must necessarily bring about the great joy of t'shuva, and the soul consequently feels the greatest natural pleasure."[1]

1.   *Orot HaT'shuva*, 5:1.

First, it is important to note the connection which Rabbi Kook makes between t'shuva and health. As we learned in Chapter Two, a healthy body is an important foundation of t'shuva. **Contrary to the picture of the penitent as a gloomy, frail, bent-over recluse who shuns the world, the true** baal t'shuva **is healthy, happy, robust, and bursting with life.**

When a person rids himself of bad habits, like overeating and cigarette smoking, his health is improved. Without these harming elements, he is stronger and more vibrant. So too, when one rids oneself of bad moral habits and base character traits, his spiritual health is improved. Without these negative influences, his soul is free to receive the flow of Divine light which fills the universe. When he is both physically and spiritually healthy, his capability to experience the Divine is enhanced. It is this "meeting with G-d" that brings the influx of joy that every baal t'shuva feels. When the unhealthy walls which had separated him from G-d are eliminated from his life, he stands ready for life's greatest discovery — the discovery that G-d and the spiritual world are real. Suddenly, G-d's love and kindness surround him. All his sins are forgiven. Instead of darkness, there is light all around him and a pool of endless love.

Rabbi Kook writes:

"In measure with every ugly thing which a person eliminates from his soul when he inwardly longs for the light of t'shuva, he discovers worlds filled with exalted illumination inside his soul. Every transgression removed is like the removal of a blindfold from the eye, and an entire horizon of vision is revealed, the light of unending expanses of heaven and earth, and all that they contain."[2]

Rabbi Yaacov Filber, in his *Commentary on Orot HaT'shuva*, points out that these new worlds are revealed **at the very moment** when a person "inwardly longs for the light of t'shuva," even before a person has been able to amend his wrongdoings.[3]

THE ULTIMATE FREEDOM

The new spiritual horizons which the *baal t'shuva* discovers give him a feeling of freedom, as if he were soaring through air. This new-found freedom comes when the walls blocking G-d's light have been razed. The *baal t'shuva* is freed from the bad habits and passions which had enslaved him in the past. He escapes from a web of wrongdoing. The lack of godliness which had pervaded his actions, his thoughts, and his being, is erased. Freed from his darkness, he can experience G-d.

"The steadfast will to always remain with the same beliefs to support the vanities of transgression into which a person has fallen, whether in deeds or in thoughts, is a sickness caused by an oppressive slavery that does not allow t'shuva's light of freedom to shine in its full strength. For it is t'shuva which aspires to the original, true freedom — Divine freedom, which is free of all bondage."[4]

Once again, we may be startled. People often think that in

2. Ibid, 5:2.
3. *Commentary on Orot HaT'shuva*, pg. 43, note 5.
4. *Orot HaT'shuva*, 5:5.

discovering G-d, one is restricting one's freedom, not expanding it. If one recognizes his Creator, he also has to recognize His laws. For a person who thinks this way, religion is perceived as a yoke of responsibility and bondage. But Rabbi Kook tells us the opposite. **The discovery of G-d is the ultimate freedom.** Finally, a person is liberated from beliefs that he held on to in order to justify his errant lifestyle. Finally, he is freed from cycles of behavior which he could not control. Like a criminal who decides to go straight, he can now put his life in line with G-d's will for the world. This is the greatest freedom!

HIGH ON T'SHUVA

Often people are afraid to set out on a course of t'shuva because they associate repentance with pain. While pain is a part of the t'shuva process, the hardships of t'shuva are quickly erased by the joy which the *baal t'shuva* discovers.

"T'shuva does not come to make life bitter, but to make it more pleasant. The happy satisfaction with life that comes with t'shuva is derived from the waves of bitterness which cling to a person during the initial stages of t'shuva. However, this is the highest, creative valor, to recognize and understand that pleasantness evolves out of bitterness, life out of the clutches of death, eternal pleasures out of sickness and pain. As this everlasting knowledge grows and becomes more clear in the mind, in the emotions, in the person's physical and spiritual natures, the person becomes a new being. With a courageous spirit, he transmits a new life force to all of his surroundings. He spreads the good news to all of his generation, and to all generations to be, that there is joy for the righteous, and that a joyous salvation is certain to come. *The humble also shall increase their joy in the L-rd, and the poorest among men shall rejoice in the Holy One of Israel.*"[5]

We will explore the connection between t'shuva and pain in more detail in Chapter Eleven. Here, it is important to note that the pain a person feels when he confronts his sins and his unholy past, is only a temporary phase of t'shuva. It resembles the pain of surgery, when a cancer must be cut out of the body. The uprooting of sin brings healing and joy in its wake, but the initial amputation is painful. It is difficult to give up the familiar, even if it be an evil habit. When a person understands this and opens himself up to change, he comes to be filled with a courageous new spirit and joy. His sins are forgiven. His life is renewed, and the world seems to be renewed with him.[6] Immediately, he wants to share his good fortune with everyone. He tells his parents with a gleam in his eyes, as if he has met the right girl. With unbounded enthusiasm, he phones his brother long distance to turn him on to the great secret which he has discovered. He is so hopped up on t'shuva, he wants the whole world to know. "Hey everybody, listen to me. You want to be happy? You want to be high? Get with it. Don't do drugs. Do t'shuva!"

RIVER OF DELIGHT

Another reason why the joy of t'shuva is so great is because the happiness of t'shuva is felt in the soul. Until a person discovers t'shuva, he experiences the pleasures of the world on the physical, emotional, or intellectual levels alone. He enjoys

5. Isaiah, 29:19; *Orot HaT'shuva*, 16:6.
6. *Sanhedrin* 97B.

good foods, stimulating books, new clothes and the like. But a man has a deeper, spiritual level of being, his soul, which derives no satisfaction from earthly pleasures.

"To what is this analogous? To the case of a city dweller who marries a princess. If he brought her all that the world possessed, it would mean nothing to her, by virtue of her being a king's daughter. So it is with the soul. If it were brought all the delights of the world, they would be nothing to it, in view of its pertaining to the higher elements."[7]

When a person does t'shuva, he opens his soul to a river of spiritual delight. The joy he discovers is like nothing which he has ever experienced. Not only are his senses affected, t'shuva touches his soul. Just as his soul is deeper than his other levels of being, the happiness he discovers is deeper. Just as his soul is eternal, his joy is eternal. Unlike the transitory pleasures of the physical world, the joy of t'shuva is everlasting. A jacuzzi feels good, but when it is over, the pleasure soon fades away. But in the heavenly jacuzzi of t'shuva, you don't just get wet — you get cleansed and transformed.

"When the light of t'shuva appears and the desire for goodness beats purely in the heart, a channel of happiness and joy is opened, and the soul is nurtured from a river of delights."[8]

This river of delight is the river of t'shuva. Rabbi Kook's use of this expression is not metaphorical alone. In the spiritual

7.   *Mesillat Yesharim*, Chapter 1, Rabbi Moshe Chaim Luzzato, Feldheim Publishers, translation by Shraga Silverstein.
8.   *Orot HaT'shuva*, 14:6.

world, there actually exists a river of t'shuva. This is the constant flow of t'shuva which, though invisible, is always present and active. It is our channel to true joy and happiness because it is our channel to G-d. Nothing in the world can compare to its pleasures.

THE REAL HERO

"Great and exalted is the pleasure of t'shuva. The searing flame of the pain caused by sin[9] purifies the will and refines the character of a person to an exalted, sparkling purity until the great joy of the life of t'shuva is opened for him. T'shuva raises the person higher and higher through its stages of bitterness, pleasantness, grieving, and joy. Nothing purges and purifies a person, raises him to the stature of being truly a man, like the profound process of t'shuva. *In the place where the baale t'shuva stand, even the completely righteous cannot stand.*"[10]

The real hero is not the Hollywood tough guy. It isn't the man who smokes Marlboro cigarettes. It isn't the corporate president who owns a Lear jet and three yachts. The true man is the person involved in t'shuva.[11] He is the person who is always seeking to better himself; the person who is always trying to come closer to G-d. He is the man who is open to self-assessment and change; the man who has the courage to

9.   For a discussion on t'shuva and the pain of sin, see Chapter Eleven of this book.

10.   *Berachot* 34B. *Orot HaT'shuva*, 13:11.

11.   *Orot HaT'shuva*, 12:2, "The more a man delves into the essence of t'shuva, he will find in it the source of heroism...." Also, *Avot*, 4:1, "Who is a hero? The man who conquers his evil inclination."

confront his soul's inner pain and to transform its bitterness into joy.

"T'shuva elevates a person above all of the baseness of the world. Notwithstanding, it does not alienate the person from the world. Rather, the *baal t'shuva* elevates life and the world with him."[12]

Sometimes, people have a misunderstanding of t'shuva. They think that t'shuva comes to separate a person from the world. While some *baale t'shuva* make a point of isolating themselves completely from secular society, this is not the ideal. During the early stages of t'shuva, a person should certainly avoid situations which are antithetical to his newfound goals, in order to rebuild his life on purer foundations, but a *baal t'shuva* is not a recluse. He should not cut himself off from the world. The opposite. By participating in the life around him, he elevates, not only himself, but also the world. After returning to G-d, he must return to the world.[13] G-d created the heavens for the angels. Our lives are to be lived down on earth. It is our task to bring healing and perfection to this world, not to the next. When the powerful life-force which went into sin is redirected

---

12. *Orot HaT'shuva*, 12:1.
13. See, *Orot HaT'shuva*, 13:4; 13:5a; 14:30, "It is precisely after being involved in a truly, pure t'shuva that one must return to the world and to life. By doing this, one returns holiness to its proper place and makes G-d's Presence sovereign in the world." See also, the book, *Arpelei Tohar* by Rabbi Kook, pg. 16, "*Tzaddikim* truly should be natural people, and every natural aspect of their bodies and beings should be characterized by life and health; then, through their spiritual greatness, they can elevate all of the world, and all things will rise up with them."

toward good, life is uplifted. A *baal t'shuva* who returns to a former situation in which he sinned, and now conducts himself in a righteous, holy manner, affects a great *tikun*. "For instance, if a man had sinful relations with a woman, and after a time was alone with her, his passion for her persisting, and his physical powers unabated, while he continued to live in the same district where he had sinned, and yet he refrains and does not transgress, he is a *baal t'shuva*."[14] He is like a gunslinger who mends his ways and comes back to town to do away with the bad guys. Because of his t'shuva, Dodge City is a better, safer, more wholesome place.

"The inner forces which led him to sin are transformed. The powerful desire which smashes all borders and brought the person to sin, itself becomes a great, exalted life-force which acts to bring goodness and blessing. The greatness of life which emanates from the highest holy source constantly hovers over t'shuva and its heroes, for they are the champions of life, who call for its perfection. They demand the victory of good over evil, and the return to life's true goodness and happiness, to the true, exalted freedom, which suits the man who ascends to his spiritual source and essential Divine image."[15]

It is time to take t'shuva out of the closet. The true champions of life are not the basketball players, not the Hollywood stars, not even the Presidents. The real heroes are the masters of t'shuva. They are the Supermen who battle the forces of darkness in order to fill the world with goodness and blessing. Teenagers! Tear down your wall posters of wrestlers and rock

14.   Rambam, *Laws of T'shuva*, 2:1.
15.   *Orot HaT'shuva*, 12:1.

stars! The people to be admired are the masters of t'shuva! You can be one too!

Chapter Eight

THOUGHTS MAKE THE MAN

THOUGHTS OF T'SHUVA

Rabbi Kook teaches that even contemplations of t'shuva have significant value. To understand this, we must look at life with a different orientation than we are used to. Usually, we are pragmatists. We judge the value of things by the influence they have on the world. For instance, ten dollars is worth more than five dollars because it can buy more. A doctorate is better than a bachelor's degree because it can lead to a better paying and more prestigious job.

There are things, however, that have an absolute value, irregardless of their tangible impact in this world. Truth is an example. Holiness is another. To this list, Rabbi Kook adds good thoughts. Contemplations of t'shuva, even if they do not lead to a resulting change in behavior, bring benefit to the individual and the world.

This is similar to the question in the Talmud — which is greater, Torah study or good deeds? The answer is Torah study because it leads to good deeds.[1] You might think that if the ultimate goal is the deeds, then they would be more important. But our Sages tell us that the thought processes which lead to the deeds is of primary concern. Being immersed in Torah has an absolute value in itself.

"The thought of t'shuva transforms all transgressions and the darkness they cause, along with their spiritual bitterness and stains, into visions of joy and comfort, for it is through these contemplations that a person is filled with a deep feeling of hatred for evil, and the love of goodness is increased within him with a powerful force."[2]

T'shuva can be dissected into two different realms. There is the nitty-gritty t'shuva of mending an actual deed, and there is the thought process which precedes the action. The value of these thoughts is not to be measured according to the activities which they inspire. For instance, a person may decide that he wants to be righteous. But when the person tries to translate this thought into action, he finds himself overwhelmed. To be righteous, he has to get up early in the morning to pray. He has to stop doing a host of forbidden deeds. He has to watch what he says, and watch what he eats. Before he even begins, his will is broken. Though his wish to do t'shuva was sincere, he couldn't find the inner strength to actualize his thoughts into deeds.

1. *Kiddushin* 40B.
2. *Orot HaT'shuva*, 7:1.

Rabbi Kook says that all is not lost. This person's original idea to do t'shuva stemmed from the deepest recesses of the soul, where it was inspired by the spiritual waves of t'shuva which encircle the world. Thus he has already been touched by t'shuva's cleansing streams. In effect, he has boarded the boat. Though his will may be weak at the moment, his soul is longing for G-d.

YOU ARE WHAT YOU THINK

"Through the contemplations of t'shuva, a person hears the voice of G-d calling him from the Torah and from the heart, from the world and all it contains. The will for good is fortified within him. The body itself, which causes transgression, becomes more and more purified until the thought of t'shuva pervades it."[3]

In the beginning of his t'shuva journey, a person must realize the absolute value of his initial inspiration. He has to find a new way of judging the value of things, not always looking for concrete benefits or results. When a person undertakes t'shuva, his thoughts weigh as much as his deeds. T'shuva is not just a process of do's and don'ts, but rather a conscious and subconscious overhaul of an individual's thought processes and emotions. Already by thinking about t'shuva one is engaged in it.

"Even the thought of t'shuva brings great healing. However, the soul can only find full freedom when this potential t'shuva is actualized. Nonetheless, since the contemplation is bound up

3.   *Orot HaT'shuva*, 7:5.

85

with the longing for t'shuva, there is no cause for dismay. G-d will certainly provide all of the means necessary for complete repentence, which brightens all darkness with its light... *A broken and contrite heart, O G-d, Thou will not despise.*"[4]

YOU HAVE A FRIEND

When we recognize the value of our thoughts, we discover a very encouraging concept. One needn't despair when confronted by the often difficult changes which t'shuva demands. This is especially true in the initial stages before a person's increasing love for G-d makes all difficulties and sacrifices seem small. **Even if a person cannot immediately redress all of his wrongdoings, he should know that there is a great value in just wanting to be good.** One can take comfort that he wants to be a better person. With G-d's help, he will also be able to actualize his yearnings. But in the meantime, just thinking good thoughts is already strengthening his inner self and the world.

This is also why t'shuva can come in a second. Just the thought of t'shuva is t'shuva itself.[5] Thoughts of t'shuva are themselves uplifting. The actual mending of activities is only a second stage. This knowledge can give a person the strength to continue through difficult times.

"To the extent that someone is aware of his transgressions, the light of t'shuva shines lucidly on his soul. Even if at the moment, he lacks the steadfastness to repent in his heart and will, the light of t'shuva hovers over him and works to renew his in-

4. Psalms, 51:19. *Orot HaT'shuva*, 7:5.
5. See Chapter Three of this book on the subject of Sudden T'shuva.

ner self. The barriers to t'shuva[6] weaken in strength, and the blemishes they cause are diminished to the degree that the person recognizes them and longs to erase them. Because of this, the light of t'shuva starts to shine on him, and the holiness of the transcendental joy fills his soul. Gates which were closed open before him, and in the end, he will achieve the exalted rung where all obstacles will be leveled. *Every valley shall be exalted, and every mountain and hill shall be made low; and the crooked shall be made straight, and the rough places plain.*"[7]

A few examples may help illustrate this idea. Individual t'shuva includes rectifying trangressions and improving character traits. Let's suppose that Joseph has stolen money from Reuven who lives two thousand miles away. At the moment, even though Joseph wants to return the money, he is unable to make the trip. This is a barrier to t'shuva. Or in a case where Reuven lives just across the street, it may be that Joseph is too embarrassed to admit his theft. Until he strengthens his will to do t'shuva, musters his inner courage, and swallows his pride, Joseph's t'shuva will be delayed. Regarding character traits, let's say that Joseph is an angry person. He is angry at his parents, at his wife and children, he is angry at his boss and at the neighbor down the street. It may take a considerable amount of introspection, and a serious course of Torah study, before he can transform his anger into love. But even if this barrier should seem insurmountable to him, he should take comfort in knowing that once the process of t'shuva has started, G-d's help is ever near.

6.   Rambam, *Laws of T'shuva*, Chapter Four.
7.   Isaiah, 40:4. *Orot HaT'shuva*, 15:7.

"When a person truly longs for t'shuva, he may be prevented by many barriers, such as unclear beliefs, physical weakness, or the inability to correct wrongs which he has inflicted on other people. The barrier may be considerable, and the person will feel remorse because he understands the weighty obligation to perfect his ways, in the most complete manner possible. However, since his longing for t'shuva is firm, even if he cannot immediately overcome all of the obstacles, he must know that the desire for t'shuva itself engenders purity and holiness, and not be put off by barriers which stand in his way. He should endeavor to seize every spiritual ascent available to him, in line with the holiness of his soul and its holy desire."[8]

In dealing with his anger, it may be that Joseph lacks the determination or courage to have a heart-to-heart talk with his boss. Or perhaps, he is afraid of losing his job. So let him begin with his parents or wife. With each step he takes, he will find greater courage for the stages ahead. And if his Pandora's Box of anger is too threatening for him to open at all, let him turn to redress other matters more in his reach, with the faith that a more complete t'shuva will come.

"One must strengthen one's faith in the power of t'shuva, and feel secure that in the thought of t'shuva alone, one perfects himself and the world. After every thought of t'shuva, a person will certainly feel happier and more at peace than he had in the past. This applies even more if one is determined to do t'shuva, and if he has made a commitment to Torah, its wisdom, and to the fear of G-d. The highest joy comes when the love of G-d

8.   *Orot HaT'shuva*, 17:2.

pulses through his being.[9] He must comfort himself and console his outcast soul, and strengthen himself in every way he can, for the word of G-d assures, *As one whom his mother comforts, so I will comfort you.*[10]

"If he discovers sins he committed against others, and his strength is too feeble to correct them, one should not despair at all, thinking that t'shuva cannot help. For the sins which he has committed against G-d and repented over, they have already been forgiven.[11] Thus, it should be viewed that the sins which are lacking atonement are outweighed by the t'shuva he was able to do. Still, he must be very careful not to transgress against anyone, and he must strive with great wisdom and courage to address all of the wrongs from the past, *Deliver thyself like a gazelle from the hand of the hunter, and like a bird from the hand of the fowler.*[12] However, let depression not overcome him because of the things he was unable to redress. Let him rather strengthen himself in the fortress of Torah, and in the service of G-d, with all of his heart, in happiness, reverence, and love."[13]

9.   Rabbi Yaacov Filber points out that these three stages of joy parallel the three stages of t'shuva deliniated in Chapter 3: physical t'shuva, religious t'shuva, and t'shuva out of a love of G-d. Filber, loc. cit. pg. 67, note 27.

10. Isaiah, 66:13.

11. Repentance and Yom Kippur alone are enough to atone for sins against G-d. Whereas to atone for sins against others, in addition to repentance and Yom Kippur, the penitent must make amends with the person he harmed. *Yoma* 85B.

12. Proverbs, 6:5.

13. *Orot HaT'shuva*, 7:6.

Even though a person has not yet been able to rectify every wrong against his fellow man, every thought of t'shuva has inestimable value. "Even the minutest measure of t'shuva awakens in the soul, and in the world, a great measure of holiness."[14] The difficulty in mending the trangressions of the past should never bring a person to despair. For even if the thought of t'shuva is still undeveloped, even if one's desire to do good contains a mixture of unrefined motives, Rabbi Kook assures us that its basic inner holiness is worth all of the wealth in the world.[15]

14.   *Orot HaT'shuva*, 14:14.
15.   Ibid.

Chapter Nine

DON'T WORRY! BE HAPPY!

THE SECRET OF STRIVING

Amongst the many eye-opening revelations on t'shuva in Rabbi Kook's writings, one concept is especially staggering in its profundity. It is such a new understanding, we have decided to devote a separate short chapter to it, to highlight its importance to the reader. Usually, we think that a process is completed when it reaches its end. We experience a feeling of satisfaction when we finish a project. An underlying tension often accompanies our work until it is accomplished. This is because the final goal is considered more important than the means.[1]

Most people feel the same way about t'shuva. Until the process of t'shuva is complete, they feel unhappy, anxious, overwhelmed with the wrongdoings which they have been unable to

---

1. See Chapter Ten of this book for a discussion on the sin of the earth, and the dichotomy it caused between the goal and the means.

redress. Rabbi Kook tells us that this perspective is wrong. When it comes to t'shuva, the goal is not the most important thing. It is the means which counts. **What matters the most is the striving for perfection, for the striving for perfection is perfection itself.**

"If not for the contemplation of t'shuva, and the comfort and security which come with it, a person would be unable to find rest, and spiritual life could not develop in the world. Man's moral sense demands justice, goodness, and perfection. Yet how very distant is moral perfection from man's actualization, and how feeble he is in directing his behavior toward the pure ideal of absolute justice. How can he aspire to that which is beyond his reach? For this, t'shuva comes as a part of man's nature. It is t'shuva which perfects him. If a man is constantly prone to transgress, and to have difficulties in maintaining just and moral ideals, this does not blemish his perfection, since **the principle foundation of his perfection is the constant longing and desire for perfection.** This yearning is the foundation of t'shuva, which constantly orchestrates man's path in life and truly perfects him."[2]

Dear reader, please note: if you are not yet a *tzaddik*, you need not be depressed. Success in t'shuva is not measured by the final score at the end of the game. It is measured by the playing. The striving for good is goodness itself. The striving for atonement is atonement. The striving for perfection is what perfects, in and of itself.

2.   *Orot HaT'shuva*, 5:6.

King Solomon teaches that no man is sin-free.[3] Transgression is part of the fabric of life. Since we are a part of this world, we too are subject to "system failure" or sin.[4] *For there is not a just man on earth that does good and never sins.*[5] Even the righteous occasionally succumb to temptation.[6] Thus, until the days of *Mashiach*,[7] an ideal, sinless existence is out of man's reach.

An illustration may help make this concept clearer. On *Yom Kippur*, we are like angels. We don't eat, we don't drink. All day long we pray for atonement from all of our sins. At the end of the day, with the final blast of the shofar, we are cleansed. But in the very next moment, as we pray the evening service, we once again ask G-d to forgive us. Forgive us for what? The whole day we have acted like angels. Our sins were whitened as snow.[8] In the few seconds between the end of *Yom Kippur* and the evening prayer, what sin did we do? Maybe at the beginning of the evening prayer, exhausted by the fast, we didn't concentrate on our words. Maybe our prayers on *Yom Kippur* were half-hearted. Maybe, we forgot to ask forgiveness for some of our sins.

The point is that the process of t'shuva never ends. Perfection in deeds is out of our reach. Thus, when a goal is unattain-

---

3. *Kohelet*, 7:20.
4. "Since nature, in its essence, lacks perception and judgment, sin is inevitable." *Orot HaT'shuva*, 5:6A. See also 6:7.
5. *Kohelet*, 7:20.
6. *Sanhedrin* 107A. Proverbs, 24:6.
7. Joel, 2:20, see Radak commentary there.
8. Isaiah, 1:18.

able, it is the striving to reach the goal that counts. Regarding t'shuva, it is the constant striving for t'shuva which purifies, enlightens, elevates, and perfects. So relax all you seekers of t'shuva. Even if you haven't yet atoned for all of your sins, DON'T WORRY. BE HAPPY. As long as you are sincerely trying, that is what really counts.

Chapter Ten

HAPPINESS NOW

THE MEANS OR THE GOAL — THAT IS THE QUESTION

As we explained in the previous chapter, people tend to place more value on the final achievement of a goal, rather than on the endeavor itself. For instance, many people focus on getting their salaries at the end of the week, rather than on their actual work. How happy they feel when the work week is over and they have their paychecks in hand! For them, their work is merely a means toward receiving their money. This phenomenon is known to cause anxiety and even depression on the job. It can even lead to accidents, when a worker, daydreaming about the future, stops paying attention to what he is doing.

If a person approaches t'shuva with this attitude, he will always focus on his shortcomings and sin, and not on his yearning and efforts to redress them. As the saying teaches, one should not focus on the half of the glass that is empty, but rather on the half which is full. Not understanding that his efforts to improve are what matter, and not the idealized vision of himself which he has not as yet achieved, he will always feel anxious, unfulfilled and forlorn.

Rabbi Kook explains that this misplacing of priorities between the means and the goal stems from the sin of the earth during the days of Creation. By understanding the depth of this teaching, we can learn to be happy, not only when we attain our goals and ideals, but also at every moment of our lives.

THE BARK AND THE FRUIT

When G-d curses Eve, the snake, and Adam in the story of Creation, the earth is cursed with them, as it says, *The earth shall be cursed on your account.*[1] The Midrash asks why. Rabbi Yehuda Bar Shalom answers that the earth transgressed G-d's command that the ground should give forth fruit trees which are fruit — not only was the fruit to be edible, the bark of the tree was supposed to be edible too, with the same taste as the fruit. The earth, however, brought forth trees which **produced** only edible fruit. The bark itself was tasteless.[2]

Rabbi Kook writes:

"At the beginning of Creation, the taste of the tree was supposed to have the same taste as the fruit. All of the means which are needed to sustain any lofty, all-encompassing spiritual goal,

1. Genesis, 3:17.
2. *Bereshit Rabbah,* 5:9.

should rightly be experienced in the soul with the same exalted pleasantness which we feel when we picture the goal itself. However, the laws of nature, along with the instability of human life, and the heaviness of the spirit when it is enclosed in a physical body, caused that only the taste of the fruit — the actualization of the final, original, ideal goal — is experienced as pleasant and sweet. The trees which produce the fruit, though they be indispensable in the growth of the fruit, have become hard, solid matter, losing their taste. This is the sin of the earth, for which it was cursed along with Adam. But every blemish is destined to be perfected. Thus we are assured, without doubt, that the time will come when the world will return to its original state, when the taste of the tree will be the same as the taste of the fruit. For the earth will return from its sin, and the necessities of practical life will no longer restrict the pleasantness of the ideal light, which is supported and brought into being by these preliminary, practical means."[3]

How is the gulf between means and the goal, between the imperfect and the ideal, to be bridged? Through t'shuva. What will cause all of the details of human endeavor and the final building to merge in pleasant harmony? T'shuva. The light of t'shuva penetrates all of the details of life, all of the stages of mending and repair, and fills them all with the taste of the final ideal.

The discrepancy in taste between the fruit of the tree and the bark represents a vast, cosmic concept. Originally, G-d intended that everything in the world would be perceived in the same deep, inner light. According to the intended plan, people would

3.   *Orot HaT'shuva*, 6:7.

have experienced every moment with the same joy as the final goal. They would have understood that the means are as important as the ideal, that all of the incompleteness and detailed work which go into achieving something are a part of the whole. With the sin of the earth, mankind lost the ability to appreciate the small things in life. People talk about the ideal future, about world peace, about universal equality, saving the environment, and the like, but the housekeeper's boycott against ozone-destroying aerosol cans is seen as something less grand. On the contrary, what joy and sense of accomplishment she should feel knowing that she is making the world a better place!

THE SECRET OF T'SHUVA

With t'shuva, the means become as vital as the goal. T'shuva penetrates all of the details of life and uplifts them to G-d. Everything is seen as important and necessary in the refinement and perfection of the existence. T'shuva enters every sphere of life, illuminating all things with the light of the future ideal, giving inspiration to all of man's work.

Rabbi Kook writes that the inner foundation of life is built upon t'shuva.[4] Material existence, he explains, is based on a step-by-step descent from Divine spiritual spheres to the worldly. Thus there is a Divine spark in everything. This spark is like the DNA of existence. When a person is involved in any detailed spark of existence, it is as if he were involved with the world itself.

---

4. *Orot HaT'shuva*, 11:4.

"When we understand to what extent the tiniest details of life, the spiritual and the physical, contain, in microcosm, all of the general laws, and that every small detail has shadows of greatness in the depths of its essence, we will no longer wonder at the secret of t'shuva which penetrates man's spirit so deeply, from the beginnings of his thoughts and beliefs, to the smallest details of his character and deeds."[5]

When we understand that every fragment is a microcosm of the whole, and that each and every person is like a world in miniature,[6] than how truly powerful is man! How influential is his each and every deed! For example, if a person stops speaking badly about other people, he not only improves himself, he improves his community. Because, he is connected to all of the cosmos, he improves all of the universe. The smallest detail of t'shuva heals man and all of existence with it! His cries for salvation echo through every realm of existence and reach the Divine throne itself. *Out of the depths, I have called to You, O L-rd.*[7] Man's every gesture of t'shuva is filled with meaning, connecting the lowest regions to the most exalted heights, the smallest details to the grandest schemes. He is the sun around which all of life orbits. His thoughts, speech, and action literally influence what will be in the world.[8]

5.   Ibid.
6.   *Zohar, Raya Mehemna, Pinchas,* Vol. 3, 257B.
7.   Psalms, 130:1.
8.   *Nefesh HaChaim,* Gate One, Chapters 3-4.

Chapter Eleven

WHO'S AFRAID OF T'SHUVA?

THE PAIN OF BIRTH

We have mentioned the bitterness and pain that accompanies the early stages of t'shuva. When people begin to enter the realm of t'shuva, they start to experience a fear, an uncertainty, an inner anguish and pain. While this unpleasant aspect of t'shuva is quickly overshadowed and forgotten in the *baal t'shuva's* pursuant great joy, it is a necessary step in the process. Recognizing its value and purging effect can help the penitent weather the stormy seas he must travel. The knowledge that the sun is shining just behind the clouds can give him the strength to continue. In the same way that a woman soon forgets the agonies of childbirth in the happiness of being a mother, the *baal t'shuva* quickly forgets the "labor pains" of t'shuva in the great joy of his rebirth.

"T'shuva does not come to embitter life, but rather to make

it more pleasant. The joy of life which comes from t'shuva evolves from the waves of bitterness which the soul wrestles with in the beginning of the t'shuva process. However, this marks the higher, creative valor which knows that sweetness stems from bitterness, life from death, eternal delight from infirmity and pain."[1]

When you first swallow aspirin tablets, there is a small taste of bitterness in the mouth. So too, in the initial stages of t'shuva, the first explorations of one's inner world can cause uncomfortable feelings. However, as one continues on the path of inner cleansing, one discovers a great happiness in knowing that he is doing what he was created to do — to get closer to G-d.

The process is not that at first you are sad and then you are happy. **Rabbi Kook teaches that you are happy from being sad.** It is the bitterness itself that causes the joy. One's suffering makes one realize that the t'shuva is sincere.

Some people are overwhelmed by the mountain of sin which seems to confront them as they begin to set their lives in order. How can they deal with so many transgressions? How can they ever make the drastic changes needed to live a holy, ethical life? Rabbi Kook reassures us that this feeling of nervousness is a very good sign. It is a sign that the person has already broken free of his previous material perspective and is ready to consider a more spiritual life.

In the same way, Rabbi Kook tell us that if you are hurting

---

1.   *Orot HaT'shuva*, 16:6.

inside, that is a sign of spiritual health. It's a sign that your inner self recognizes that it does not belong to an environment of sin. Feeling pain over the sins of the past is an important part of the t'shuva process.[2] It goes hand-in-hand with a commitment to a life of good deeds in the future.[3]

The pain and anxiety associated with the first thoughts of t'shuva evolve, in part, from the need to separate from former ways. Just as an operation to remove a cancerous tumor from the body is accompanied by pain, so too is t'shuva. However, the pain is a sign that a healing process is underway. An amputation hurts, but sometimes it is needed to save a person's life. Before the operation, the patient is wary. His leg may be gangrene, but it still is his leg. What will he be like without it? Will he be the same man? How will he function?

These are all natural, legitimate, and very distressing questions. The unknown can be scary. So too, when a person has become used to a part of his psyche, even if it be some negative trait which is detrimental to his inner well-being, it is not easy to escape from its clutches. Already it has become a citizen of his soul. Breaking away from the past and being open to change is not a simple task. Great inner courage is needed. Often, it can only be done with the help of a teacher or guide.[4] In effect, in unveiling the step-by-step process of t'shuva, Rabbi Kook is giving us a map to assist us on the way.

"The pain experienced upon the initial thought of t'shuva

2. Rambam, *Laws of T'shuva*, 2:4.
3. Ibid, 2:2.
4. *Mesillat Yesharim*, Ch. 3.

derives from the severance from evil dispositions which cannot be corrected while they are organically attached to the person and damaging all of his being. T'shuva uproots the evil aspects of the spirit and returns it to its original essence. Every separation causes pain, like the amputation of a diseased organ for medical purposes. However, it is through these deep inner afflictions that a person is freed from the dark bondage of his sins and base inclinations, and from all of their bitter influences."[5]

CHEESEBURGERS

Let's say a person wants to do away with a tendency to get angry. He realizes that his temper is a negative trait. He sees that it causes both himself and other people harm. But he is so accustomed to reacting with anger when things don't go his way, he finds it very difficult to change. Anger has become a part of his personality. It's one of the tools that he uses to deal with the world. It is so much a part of him, he often walks around with a scowl on his face. Thus, to give up this part of his character would involve a real loss. Since loss causes grief and frustration, his efforts to give up his anger make him even angrier than he was at the start. He fears that parting with his anger will leave him utterly defenseless. This feeling frustrates him even more until he is ready to really explode.

Another example will help us understand the pain that is associated with loss. The lover of cheeseburgers who realizes that he has to give up his favorite food to comply with the Jewish dietary laws will feel a sense of great stress. He lives on cheeseburgers. He loves cheeseburgers. All of his free time is

5.   *Orot HaT'shuva*, 8:1.

centered around cheeseburgers. At his early stage of t'shuva, before he has encountered the ecstasy of discovering G-d and Torah, his sense of spiritual delight is not so keenly developed that he can easily do away with the material pleasure which cheeseburger-eating provides. Thus the very thought that cheeseburgers will no longer be a part of his life causes him pain.

While the example of an amputation helps us understand the pain of separation, a distinction between amputation and t'shuva must be made. Amputation removes all of the malignant limb, whereas t'shuva removes only the cancer.[6] The cut of t'shuva is clean. No good cells are lost. After the incision is made, and a person decides to free himself from all of the negative aspects surrounding his soul, after he makes the cut, no organ is missing. Just the opposite occurs. He has gained in the process. Cut loose from the shackles of sin, he discovers incredible new energy and strength in cleaving to G-d.

Thus, when a person approaches t'shuva, the very first stage involves saying good-bye to some of his old emotional and psychological buddies, and this naturally causes remorse.

FEAR OF RETRIBUTION

In addition to the pain caused by fears of separation and change, when a person begins a process of honest introspection into his spiritual life, a great fear of retribution arises. Confronting the darkness of his life, he is terrified of the blinding light at the end of the tunnel. He feels naked, sullen with sin, guilty,

6.   *Orot HaT'shuva*, 9:10.

and deserving of punishment. Frightened, he often turns away. Terrified of the ghosts that he has discovered, he slams down the lid of the chest. He continues in his old ways, unchanged. Even though his sins are hurting him inside, the familiar pain, he decides, is more comfortable than the retribution he deserves. Yet if he had only gone forward, he would have discovered that the great light which frightened him was not the fire of Hades, but rather G-d's transcendental kindness, which is always waiting to embrace the returnee with the gift of His love.

In analyzing the angst associated with t'shuva, Rabbi Kook reveals that this pain does not stem from the prospect of retribution, as the person believes, but rather from the pain of the soul itself.

"The great pains which fill the psyche at the thought of t'shuva, even though it sometimes seems that they are caused by the fear of retribution, are in truth, the sufferings of the soul because it is infested with sin, a state of being which is contrary to its pure, spiritual essence. It is these sufferings themselves, however, which cleanse the soul. The person who inwardly recognizes the treasure of goodness contained in these pains, accepts them with absolute love and peace of mind. In this way, he is elevated to many new heights; the Torah he learns stays with him; and his character is perfected. The effects of his sins on his soul are not only erased, but actually transformed into harbingers of good, radiating with a spiritual splendor."[7]

Thus the fear and pain which people initially encounter when they set out on the journey of t'shuva stems from several

7. *Orot HaT'shuva*, 8:2.

different causes, one deeper than the next. First, there is the fear of change and with having to part with old ways. Then there is a deeper fear of G-d's punishment. However, Rabbi Kook explains that this fear of hell is really a projection. It is not the pain of purgatory which is felt, but rather the pain of sin itself. Sin is anathema to the soul. It is not an inherent part of man's constitution. The soul is revolted by sin. It cries out in anguish. Unable to cope with his spiritual pain, man projects his inner turmoil onto something else, something outside of his life, onto little red devils and the torments of hell. This helps him to live with himself, to cover up the teeming spider nest inside him and say, "I'm really OK. It is G-d and His nasty devils who have the problem."

THE DISHARMONY OF SIN

Delving one step deeper, Rabbi Kook explains that the pain of sin results from the disharmony it causes between the soul and the essential goodness of life and the universe. Because an individual's soul is attached to the soul of all existence, when a person falls into the darkness of sin, his soul is cut off from the positive Divine plan for the world and it experiences the pain of exile.

"Every transgression torments the heart because it severs the unity between the individual and all of existence... The basis of the pain which he feels does not stem from the specific transgression itself, but from the deeper essence of the sin which has alienated the soul from the natural order of life, which radiates with a Divine moral light that fills all of the world with unity and higher purpose."[8]

Rabbi Kook tells us that the true underlying pain of sin does not come from, for example, feeling remorse over having stolen, but from the alienation from G-d which the sin causes. An individual's sins cut him off from the symphony of Creation. While the world is progressing forward on a developmental path of elevation and perfection, his sins are taking him backward. All of society, culture, medicine, and general human endeavor are going forward, improving, becoming more moral, and he is enmeshed in sin. It may be that the individual is unaware of this spiritual imbalance, but his soul feels rent asunder. It senses its disharmony, disunity, and disconnection from life's ongoing yearning for justice and goodness. Severed from the inner, spiritual dimension of life, a person suffers anxiety, anguish, and loneliness, in the many forms they take, including depression, neuroses, and disease. Though he may surround himself with hundreds of people, though he occupy himself day and night with business, family, and pleasure, he is a secretly tormented soul, a revolver ready to go off.

The remedy, Rabbi Kook teaches, is t'shuva. Only t'shuva can reconnect the sinner with G-d. Only t'shuva can restore the harmony between a man's soul and the world. Only t'shuva can wipe away the sins which prevent a man from being a positive contributor to life.[9]

8.   Ibid, 8:3.
9.   Ibid. See also, *Orot HaT'shuva*, 8:7.

MEN IN BLACK

Should an individual choose a life of sin, G-d forbid, rather than a life of t'shuva, a terrible darkness envelops his soul, and his thoughts, aspirations, and character become seeped in evil. These people are the wicked of the world who see the world in the dark colors which mirror their soul. These are the cynics who find fault in everything, the irreverent who complain against G-d.[10]

Lacking the will to escape his dungeon of sin, cut off from the world's future of goodness, the wicked cower behind defensive masks of scorn. They are like the sour notes of a symphony, the coughs in the theater, the laughter in the balcony, the Nietzches and Nazis of the world, who condemn the ideals which they cannot obtain. Too weak to escape the clutches of sin, they become its propounders.

The fear that accompanies the awakenings of t'shuva is what keeps people imprisoned in darkness. It is a fear that grips whole nations. Rather than acknowledge that their cultures are based on falsehood and evil, entire civilizations cling to their delusions and myths. Instead of embracing the light of G-d, the world pays mere lip service, hiding behind one brand of paganism or another.[11]

---

10. Ibid, 8:3.
11. See the book, *War and Peace*, Torat Eretz Yisrael Publications, Chapters 5 and 8.

WE CAN ALL BE RIGHTEOUS!

Existential pain is not only experienced by those far from G-d, but also by the righteous. A *tzaddik* who dedicates his whole life to fostering goodness, can also fall out of harmony with existence. Because his soul is so sensitive to evil, he reacts to every small transgression with grief and despair. Perhaps his intention in doing a good deed was not on the proper level. Perhaps he failed to maintain concentration throughout all of his prayers. To the extent that he fails to be pure in all of his actions, emotions, and thoughts, his soul experiences and calls out for t'shuva. He longs to be closer to G-d, to be reunited with the harmony of existence.[12]

Rabbi Kook explains that the pain of the righteous person stems not only from his own personal shortcomings. Even if he were to be sinless, he would still feel the pain of the universal soul as it longs for a higher connection to G-d. Because of the unity of all existence, as long as the world is darkened with sin, the *tzaddik* suffers too. He feels the absence of Divine light in the world, and the pain of the exiled *Shekhina*.[13] He carries the pain of the world in his soul, and he expresses, with all of his being, all of his organs, all of his strength, the world's longing for G-d. Because he embodies the sufferings of the world, when he is forgiven, the world is forgiven with him.[14]

---

12. *Orot HaT'shuva*, 8:5.
13. *Taanit* 16A. See also, *Noam Elimelech, Parshat Shmot*, last paragraph.
14. *Orot HaT'shuva*, 8:6. Of interest is the verse, Isaiah 53:4, which the Christians maintain is referring to their messiah. The verse however, when studied with the text which surrounds it, is clearly referring to the nation of Israel: *But in truth, he has borne our sicknesses and endured*

Rabbi Kook has further good news. We all can be righteous!

"Every person who deeply feels the remorse of t'shuva and the inner turmoil to redress his wrongdoings, both those which he can readily mend, and those which he hopes to address, with G-d's help, in the future — he should include himself with the righteous whose thoughts of t'shuva renew the entire world with a new light."[15]

Rabbi Yaacov Filber, in his study of *Orot HaT'shuva*, explains that a person should aim to be **precisely** like those *tzaddikim* who renew the world with a new light. These are the *tzaddikim* who long for, not only personal completion, but even more fervently, for the perfection of all of the world.[16]

NO NEED FOR DESPAIR

Rabbi Kook's level after level exploration into the psychology of sin does not end in despair, but in peace and salvation. Rabbi Kook explains that the despair a person feels when he confronts his sins is itself a source of hope. **The fact that a person is in a state of pain and despair means that he senses his alienation from the positive forces of life.** He realizes that sin is not the ideal. This means that the light of morality and holi-

---

our pains.... Israel is the true "world *tzaddik*" who atones for all of mankind. See the Debate of the Ramban against Pablo Christiani, *The Writings of the Ramban*, Mosad HaRav Kook.

15. *Orot HaT'shuva*, 8.6.

16. Filber, pg. 76, nt. 27. See also, *Mesillat Yesharim*, Chapter 19, on the righteous who suffer over the lack of G-d's honor in the world. Also, *Noam Elimelech, Parshat Shmot*, last paragraph.

ness in his soul still flickers. In his innermost heart, he still longs for goodness. All is not lost. The important thing is not to fall prey to despair, and to remember that a great happiness is on the way.[17]

"When an individual contemplates embarking on a course of total t'shuva, of mending all of his feelings and deeds, even if this is only a thought, he must not be discouraged by the feelings of fear which arise when he faces his many sins, which now seem so pronounced. This is only natural, for as long as a person is seized by the baser side of his nature, and by the dark, negative traits which surround him, he does not feel the weight of his sins so strongly. Occasionally, he feels nothing, and fancies himself a *tzaddik*. But since his moral sense is awakening, the light of his soul immediately is revealed, and it probes all of his being and exposes all of his wrongs. Then his heart shudders with great fear over his lowliness and lack of perfection. But it is exactly at this instant that he should feel that this awareness, and the worry it causes, are the best signs, forecasting a complete salvation through self-perfection, and he should strengthen himself through this recognition in the L-rd his G-d."[18]

While pain is a necessary part of the t'shuva process, a person must be very careful not to let the pain of sin turn into depression to the extent that it weakens the will for t'shuva. Otherwise, Rabbi Kook warns, depression may spread like a cancer throughout the body and soul. One must always keep in mind the purging affects of spiritual pain and remember that the

---

17. *Orot HaT'shuva*, 8:15.
18. Ibid, 8:16.

light of atonement is already working to return the soul to its natural state of joy.[19] Even the physical and psychic pains that often cause a person to be more introspective, whether it be disease, the loss of a loved one, or a setback in business, these too can be the springboards of t'shuva.

DEPRESSION — THE SOURCE OF JOY

Ironically, depression prepares the way for the joy which the *baal t'shuva* discovers. To understand this deep concept, we have to understand that it is the sense of G-d's majestic perfection which causes sin to be so intolerable. When a person is aware that his sadness over his sins results from the Divine light working on his soul — this recognition brings unparalleled joy and satisfaction. He feels that G-d is with him! He senses G-d's presence! This is the spiritual happiness which accompanies the feeling of depression in the heart of the *baal t'shuva*. Thus the pain and melancholy which a person experiences because of his sins is, in fact, the wonderful sign that G-d has already turned toward him to bring him healing and joy.[20]

Rabbi Kook discusses another source of the pain of t'shuva. When the light of t'shuva embraces a person, he is enveloped by a spirit of holiness and purity. His soul fills with a passionate love of G-d, and he longs for a life of honesty and moral upliftment. However, at the same time that this "born again" feeling radiates through his being, he is still trapped in the pathways of sin, and he doesn't know how to escape from his darkness and embark on a new way of life. This frustration

19.   Ibid, 8:12.
20.   Ibid, 15:9.

113

causes pain. Yet, the very fact that a person experiences this anguish is itself the gateway to happiness.

"The will to be good, this, in itself, is a Divine wind from *Gan Eden*, which blows on the soul and fills it with infinite joy, to the extent that the hellish flames of deep anguish are transformed into rivers of delight."[21]

A TOTAL BAAL T'SHUVA

The appellation *baal t'shuva*, or master of t'shuva, suggests a person who has successfully reached the end of the process and mastered all of its facets. Rabbi Kook, however, tells us that this is not the case at all. **If a person is broken and shattered with remorse because of his sins, he is a master of t'shuva already.**

"If a person has such a low estimation of himself that the great bitterness in his soul, his fallen moral state, and his sins, prevent him from studying Torah and observing the commandments, from engaging in work, and interacting with people with a calm, healthy happiness, then he must believe in his heart that in feeling such depression over his sins, he is certainly, at that very moment, a total *baal t'shuva*. Accordingly, he has already elevated his being, and he can set his mind at rest and return to being happy and cheerful, occupying himself with goodness

---

21. *Orot HaT'shuva*, 16:3. See Rabbi Yaakov Filber's *Commentary on Orot HaT'shuva*, pg. 207, note 24. Also, Chapter Thirteen of this book, regarding the power of the will.

in a peaceful and joyous disposition, for G-d is good and just."[22]

REMORSE

One of the main aspects of t'shuva is remorse.[23] Rabbi Kook compares remorse to a flame. On the one hand, fire destroys what it contacts, while on the other hand, it gives off light and warmth.[24] In a similar manner, the pain of remorse purges away the sins of the past, while stirring a person to a healthier, more constructive life in the future. Just as a brushfire is used to clear a field of thorns to make way for new planting, remorse clears the slate of our lives, and prepares the foundation for new growth and new life — a life filled with goodness and Torah.

"The flame of remorse, when it appears in a sensitive soul through the torchlight of t'shuva, is a holy fire, a fire filled with light and warmth, filled with life. When it falls on a pure spirit, on a soul alive and illuminated with the light of grace and intelligence endowed with holy knowledge, then it is transformed into a vibrant and powerful force, an active force which cleanses and purifies, which increases courage and strength, forges pathways, and grants new spiritual power to all spheres of existence. It brings with it a new awakening filled with new life. The person becomes a new creation, refined and made pure, with a vision toward the heights, toward the loftiest horizons of knowledge and understanding, which, in turn, inspires a longing for t'shuva.

---

22. *Orot HaT'shuva*, 14:23.
23. Rambam, *Laws of T'shuva*, 2:3.
24. See, Filber, pg. 147, note 37.

"Rays of light will come to him from the light of *Mashiach*, from the root of the Torah and all of the commandments, from all of the good deeds and all of the character traits, to illuminate his dark paths and his barren ways. And together with his own building, he will build an edifice for the world, and many will walk by his light, which at first was lit for himself — a light for one and for a multitude of people, *And thou shalt be called, the repairer of the breach, the restorer of paths to dwell in.*"[25]

THE TRUE HEROES

Simply put, to the initiate, the pain that comes with t'shuva is scary. While many people look at the *baal t'shuva* as an insecure person who has run away from the challenges of life, the very opposite is true. The *baal t'shuva* is the man of courage. He is the true hero. He is the one prepared to set out on the greatest journey in life. He begins by saving himself and ends up by saving the world.

---

25.   Isaiah, 58:12. *Orot HaT'shuva*, 13:12.

Chapter Twelve

SUCCESS

THE KEY TO SUCCESS

It is no secret that western society is success oriented. Everyone wants to be a success, whether it be a successful basketball player, a successful lawyer, a successful doctor, a successful housewife... the list goes on and on. Success is championed as one of life's greatest values. Everyone loves success stories. Everyone envies successful people. From the earliest ages, children are taught to admire success. Parents push their kids to be successful. The drive to succeed is reinforced in schools. The competition is fierce to get into top colleges, because they are seen as the doors to success. Working your way up the ladder of success is the mainstay of capitalism. Accordingly, bookstores are filled with guides on how to succeed.

All of this means that the poor soul who does not succeed is a loser. In western society, if you are not a success, you are probably very unhappy. Your self-image is bound to be low. The successful people are the winners, and you are nothing more than a bum.

Rabbi Kook has good news. If you are a loser, all is not lost. You too can be a winner. You too can succeed. How? Through t'shuva.

That's right. **The key to success is t'shuva.** For when life is looked at through spiritual glasses, the most important thing is neither money, nor honor, nor power, nor fame. The most important thing is being a good person. True success lies in simply striving to be good. For real achievement is measured by what is important to G-d, not by what society flaunts. In G-d's eyes, a woman can be successful without looking like Barbie. A man can be a success without having five or six credit cards and a six-figure salary. The real man, the real success, is the man of t'shuva, the man of Torah.

THE WILL TO BE GOOD

Rabbi Kook discusses this startling idea in his writings on *ratzon*, רצון. The Hebrew word *ratzon* is usually translated as will, or willpower, but the word has a deep connotation which requires some further explanation.

"The will which is forged by t'shuva is the will which is imbedded in the depths of life, and not the lesser will that concerns itself with the superficial and external facets of life. This (deeper) will is the most fundamental force in the foundation of life, and this is the genuine character of the soul."[1]

This fundamental force is the desire to get closer to G-d. This is the deepest expression of the will. For instance, the desire to eat ice cream is a relatively superficial desire, an offshoot of the desire to eat. On a deeper level, the desire to eat is an expression of the will to survive. While not every man has a desire to eat ice cream, every man does have a will to survive. This will, the will to live, is a deeper phase of *ratzon*, and something less dependent upon a man's free choice. This can be seen in an old, dying person. Though racked with sufferings, he still clutches onto life with his last ounce of strength. Even if he lapses into a coma, the will to live in his soul continues to function.

On an even deeper level, buried in the will to live is man's deepest, most basic will — the will to get close to G-d. The will to be connected to G-d finds expression in the will to do good and in the longing for goodness. Just as G-d is good,[2] we should be good. Just as G-d is giving, we should be giving.[3] Man is the only creature who possesses a free will.[4] Our task is to align our will with the will of our Creator.[5] For the Jewish people, living a life of goodness means living a life filled with Torah,[6]

---

1.   *Orot HaT'shuva*, 9:1.
2.   Psalms, 45:8; 136:1; 145:9.
3.   Rambam, *Sefer HaMitzvot, Mitzvah* 8.
4.   Rambam, *Laws of T'shuva*, 5:1.
5.   Avot, 2:4.
6.   Ibid, 6:3.

which is G-d's will for the Jews.[7] This is our true happiness, as it says, *The statutes of the L-rd are right, rejoicing the heart.*[8]

The Torah represents the Divine good, as expressed in a code of behavior on earth. One can readily understand that a person gets closer to G-d by doing what He ordains. When a man attaches his will to G-d's, his will is uplifted toward a higher ideal. He doesn't merely want to make a good living, come home, open a beer, and watch TV. His life is more idealistically oriented. He tends to think less of himself and he longs to help everyone he can.

In a similar light, sin acts as a barrier between man and his Maker.[9] When a person defies G-d's will, he distances himself from G-d. He falls out of harmony with existence, because all of existence is doing G-d's will. The sun rises every day just as G-d has decreed. Rains fall, flowers grow, birds chirp, all in harmony with G-d's will. Only man has the freedom to turn his will against G-d.[10]

If a person's will to do good slips off the right path, he quickly comes to transgress.[11] Rabbi Kook explains that every sin weakens the will to do good. With a weakened moral desire, a man can fall into the clutches of sin completely, G-d forbid.

This severence from G-d can only be cured by t'shuva. It

7.   Deut., 10:12.
8.   Psalms, 19:9.
9.   *Sefer Maor VaShemesh, Parshat Tavoh,* paragraph beginning *Ha'ish.*
10. Rambam, *Laws of T'shuva,* 5:1.
11. Interestingly, the Hebrew word for sin, חטא, means missing the mark.

is through t'shuva that man recognizes the value of goodness. This recognition strengthens the will to do good. The more a person learns about the goodness of G-d, and the more he learns Torah, the more he wants to come closer to G-d.[12] Concurrently, when he prays to come closer to G-d, his will for goodness is fortified. Standing before his Maker in prayer, he nullifies his will before G-d's will. Attached once again to the Divine "superwill" for the world, he finds the inner resources and power to turn his evil inclination toward the good. In this manner, his sins are transformed into merits.

THE EVER-RAGING BATTLE

The constant spiritual battle between the evil inclination and the good inclination is a part of the inner fabric of life. As the book *Mesillat Yesharim* makes clear, all of this world is a testing ground.[13] Will a man follow his will to do good, or will he be led astray after sin? The hero, the winner, is the man who clings to G-d in all of his doings. This is success.

"The Holy One Blessed be He has put man in a place where the factors which draw him further from the Blessed One are many. These are the earthy desires which, if he is pulled after them, cause him to be drawn further from and to depart from the true good. It is seen, then, that man is veritably placed in the midst of a raging battle... If he is valorous, and victorious on all sides, he will be the "whole man," who will succeed in uniting with his Creator, and he will leave the corridor to enter the palace, to glow in the light of life. To the extent that he has

---

12. *Eicha Rabbah, Petichta,* 2.
13. *Mesillat Yesharim,* Chapter One.

subdued his evil inclination and his desires, and withdrawn from those factors which draw him further from the good, and exerted himself to become united with it, to that extent he will attain and rejoice in the light of life.

"If you look more deeply into the matter, you will see that the world was created for man's use. In truth, man is the center of a great balance. For if he is pulled after the world and is drawn further from his Creator, he is damaged, and he damages the world with him. And if he rules over himself and unites himself with his Creator, and uses the world only to aid him in the service of his Creator, he is uplifted and the world itself is uplifted with him."[14]

A WORLD UPSIDE DOWN

Success, we see, is achieved in life when one channels his will towards goodness. What makes this simple teaching so startling? Precisely because it stands in conflict with all of modern western culture. Today, who are the "successful people"? The movie stars and rock stars, the millionaires, the famous artists, the political leaders, the sports heroes. These are society's champions. These are the role models whom young people emulate. They are considered successful because they have successfully pursued and attained honor, power, money and fame — values which Judaism places at the negative side of the scale of character traits. Our Sages teach that we should flee from honor and pride.[15] Our prophets tell us that it is not the pow-

---

14. *Mesillat Yesharim*, Chapter One, Feldheim Publishers, translated by Shraga Silverstein.
15. Avot, 4:21; 6:6.

erful and egotistical who shall inherit the earth, but the humble and righteous.[16] The Midrash teaches that someone who seeks fame will lose it,[17] and that the pursuit of wealth brings misery in its wake.[18] In other words, chances are that the faces we see in this world on the cover of People Magazine are not the faces which we are going to see in Heaven in the world to come.

Modern western culture encourages man to channel his will toward the more negative aspects of life. Society's passions and pulls are so powerful that a person soon loses sight of what's good, and begins to glorify and worship the bad. The push toward success is so great, everything becomes permissible in the fight to achieve it. Vice becomes an acceptable norm. The will for goodness, man's most basic desire, is shackled in sin. Only the power of t'shuva can save it.

Rabbi Kook writes:

"The constant focus of a person's thoughts on t'shuva builds a person's character on a noble foundation. He constantly fills himself with a sensitive spirit, which places him on the spiritual foundation of life and existence.

16. Psalms, 37:11.
17. *Tanchuma, Vayikra* 3.
18. *Avot,* 2:7. *Eruvin* 13B. Generally speaking, what the world holds in high esteem is often quite rotten. This is the message of Rabbi Yehoshua ben Levi who visited Heaven in a trance and saw a world upside down, where the rich and important of this world were the least honored, and the poor and humble were on the top of the ladder of success, *Pesachim* 50A. And see *Baba Batra* 10A, regarding R. Yosef, the son of R. Yehoshua.

"When t'shuva constantly fills the heart, it reinforces in the person the great value of a spiritual life, and reinforces in him the great foundation that a good will is everything. All of the talents in the world are merely to implement the person's will to do good, which becomes stamped into his being through the light of constant t'shuva. A great influx of G-d's spirit falls constantly over him, and a holy will increases in him, far surpassing the aspirations of ordinary men. He comes to recognize the positive value of true success — the will for goodness, which is solely dependent on the person himself, and not on any external condition."[19]

Thus it is t'shuva which strengthens a person's longing for goodness. It is t'shuva which gives him the spiritual light to break free from the darkness of sin. It is t'shuva which revitalizes and restores his good will. When the spiritual world opens before him, he realizes that talents are not ends in themselves, but the means in serving G-d. One realizes that the goal is not just to be a good singer, but to sing the praises of G-d. The goal is not just to be a good writer, but to use one's talent as a writer to bring people closer to G-d. The greatness of one's talent is not the measure of success, but rather the direction it takes. Nor is public reknown always the yardstick. Rabbi Aryeh Levin, the "*Tzaddik* of Jerusalem,"[20] lived a life of one good deed after another, but outside of Israel, he was hardly known at all. **Who in G-d's eyes do you think was a greater success, Rabbi Aryeh Levin or Frank Sinatra, who was known all over**

---

19. *Orot HaT'shuva*, 9:1.
20. See the book, *A Tzaddik in our Time,* by Simcha Raz, Feldheim Publishers, Jerusalem.

the world? The answer is obvious when we judge our lives by Jewish standards, and not by the standards of western culture.

Rabbi Kook teaches that by attaching oneself to G-d's will for the world, he brings his life into harmony with the positive flow of existence.[21] In the process, a person's own willpower is fantastically strengthened for he has plugged himself into the Source of all sources, the Power of all powers, the Will of all wills, the King of all kings. People who attain this level possess a super-human energy and drive. Our forefather, Yaakov, went years with almost no sleep.[22] King David would sleep only a tiny portion of the night.[23] *Tzaddikim* like Rabbi Aryeh Levin, Rabbi Kook, Rabbi Moshe Feinstein, and the *Rebbe* of Chabad, were known to fill up all of their days, their evenings, and their nights with endless study, teaching, meetings, prayer and good deeds. The person who is strengthened by a holy will, and an influx of G-d's spirit, comes to know that the zenith of success is in channeling one's will toward goodness, and that this, **in and of itself,** is the highest attainment in life, independent of his status in society, and other external factors such as honor and fame.

"This success is the greatest happiness, greater than all other treasures. Only this success brings joy to the whole world and all of existence. For a good will which is always active in the soul transforms all of life toward goodness."[24]

21. *Orot HaT'shuva*, 9:1.
22. Genesis, 31:40.
23. *Succah* 26B.
24. *Orot HaT'shuva*, 9:1.

Thus we learn that the striving to be a good person is the key to success and true happiness — to a happiness centered in G-d. A happiness which a man acquires, not only in this world, but also in the world to come, where money, and honor, and fame don't really matter at all.[25] As the expression goes — you can't take it with you.[26]

Interestingly, Rabbi Kooks says that when a person's will is purified through t'shuva, the happiness and goodness he discovers is not limited to himself, but rather, the happiness and goodness released from the bondage of sin fills the whole world. This is because, on the deepest level, the individual's will for goodness is derived from the universal will for goodness which G-d has placed in the world. In strengthening his personal longing for goodness, he magnifies the will for good in existence as a whole.[27]

"T'shuva elevates a person above all of the baseness which exists in the world, but it does not estrange him from the world. To the contrary, he elevates the world and life with him. The forces which caused him to sin are purified in him. The powerful will which pierces all boundaries and caused him to sin is transformed into a positive force that brings great good and blessing. The nobility of life, stemming from the yearning for the realm of the holy, surrounds the heroes of t'shuva. They are the elite of existence, who call out for its perfection, for the victory over obstacles, for the return to true goodness and joy. They call out for the return to the exalted heights of true freedom, which

25. *Mesillat Yesharim*, Chapter One. *Pesachim* 50A; *Baba Batra* 10A.
26. Psalms, 49:17-18, Ecclesiastes, 5:14.
27. *Yoma* 86B. For a similar idea, see the Rambam, *Laws of T'shuva*, 3:3.

befit a person who rises heavenward in accordance with his spiritual source and his foundation in G-d's image."[28]

In setting one's will on a course of t'shuva, in freeing oneself from the shackles of sin, from false idols, and from the illusions of worldly success, man discovers an incomparable happiness and nobility which extends beyond a person's own life to elevate all of existence.

28.   *Orot HaT'shuva*, 12:1. Genesis, 1:27.

Chapter Thirteen

THE POWER OF THE WILL

THE WILL TO GOODNESS

We have learned that t'shuva is the force which makes the world go round. Just as gravity keeps us here on earth, t'shuva keeps us longing for the heavens. For the individual, the source of this force lies in his or her willpower. The will is the battery of t'shuva. For a person to be healthy, happy, and in harmony with the universe, his will must be freed from the bondage of sin and directed toward goodness and G-d.

We are not accustomed to thinking in terms of the will. In school we learn about many different subjects, we learn about different professions, we learn how to get along in the world. But we don't learn very much about being good. Rabbi Kook, however, teaches that education should focus not on professional training alone, but on finding ways to direct all of man's endeavors, both material and spiritual, toward the world's general aspiration for goodness.[1]

"Pure honesty demands that all of the labor of science should be directed toward the fundamental ideal of enhancing man's will with the ultimate goodness fitting to it, to refine the will, to strengthen it, to sanctify it, to purify it, to habituate it through educational channels to always strive for what is lofty and noble."[2]

When, however, mankind strays from the proper course, and instead of striving to elevate the will, leaves it wallowing in its baseness, wanting only to satisfy the will's lower passions, then humanity plunges into darkness, degeneracy, and idolatry.

"Out of its depths, (mankind) will cry out to the G-d of truth and return to the holy goal of making the foundation of every activity the uplifting of the will.... This is the entire basis of t'shuva, the elevation of the will, transforming it to good, to rise up from darkness to light, from a valley of tribulation to a gateway of hope."[3]

SHOT OUT OF A CANNON

In Chapter Three, we saw that t'shuva can come about gradually, or in a sudden powerful flash. Gradual t'shuva resembles any developmental, step-by-step process whereby one thing leads to another in a natural fashion like the growth of

1. *Orot HaT'shuva*, 15:2.
2. Ibid.
3. Ibid.

a tree, which progresses from the seed to the fruit in a slow, predictable process.

Sudden t'shuva is different. It seems to come about all at once with superhuman energy and willpower. Where does this great thrust of life energy come from? If we had spiritual glasses to analyze the process, what catalysts and forces would we see?

The longing for goodness that makes up a person's will-power has a resiliency like that of a spring. Sin causes the will for goodness to be contracted, like a spring which is being stepped on. The further a person is caught up in sin, the tighter the spring is compressed. When a person frees himself from the shackles of sin, he is freeing his willpower to return to cleaving to G-d. Since his willpower was in such a constricted state, when it is released, it explodes with a super momentum and force, far greater than the force of gradual t'shuva. The sudden *baal t'shuva* has a magnificent outburst of will which propels him into a frenzy of spiritual endeavor. From the depth of his darkness, he discovers an incredible light, an incredible good-ness. All at once, BOOM, he is turned on by G-d. His prayer, his Torah study, his good deeds are all filled with a fiery in-tensity and fervor for universal good.[4]

It is this revitalized energy which makes the newly reli-gious seem "born again." This occurs because his willpower has been rescued and recharged. This accounts for the teaching that a *tzaddik* cannot reach the level of a *baal t'shuva*,[5] for a *tzaddik*

4.   *Orot HaT'shuva*, 9:3.
5.   *Berachot* 34B.

is motivated by the normal, step-by-step will to do good, and not by the explosive, shot-out-of-a-cannon passion of the *baal t'shuva*.

Just as the completely righteous cannot stand in the same place where the *baale t'shuva* stand,[5] so are ordinary *baale t'shuva* unable to stand in the place of *baale t'shuva* who stubbornly overcome difficult obstacles.[6]

THE HEALING SCALPEL OF T'SHUVA

Because of its great power, Rabbi Kook warns that t'shuva, if misused, can become a lethal weapon. Like a surgical knife, t'shuva can be the key to new healthy life, or to self-destruction.

"When one contracts the will, when one represses the life-force through an inner course of abstention out of the desire to avoid all transgression, a contraction of the will for goodness also occurs. The power of the moral side of life is also lessened. A man engaged in purifying his life suffers a weakness like that of a sick person who was cured by electric shock therapy, which wiped out the disease, but also weakened his healthy life-force."[7]

---

6. *Orot HaT'shuva*, 15:8.
7. *Orot HaT'shuva*, 9:10. Rabbi Kook writes here that this purifying, yet weakening, relationship is particularly active during the days devoted to t'shuva leading up to *Rosh Hashana* and *Yom Kippur*. This penitential season is therefore followed by the joyous holidays of *Sukkot* and *Simchat Torah* to restore a person's healthy life-force and complete the t'shuva process. See also, *Orot HaT'shuva*, 9:4.

The first stages of t'shuva effect a person's willpower in a negative fashion. Usually, the *baal t'shuva* consciously restricts his worldly desires. All feelings which border on lust are rejected, along with every strong passion, including many positive ones such as feelings of happiness, warmth, and love. Fearing sin, he may decide to limit all of his physical needs, since everything that he is accustomed to doing seems wrong. He becomes passive, lethargic and weak.

Of course, when the will has become addicted to unhealthy passions, it must be restricted to tame its hungry roar. **But when a person cuts down on his life-force by slamming on the brakes, not only his bad habits come to a stop, he also neutralizes the good.** This happens because the will, or the life-force, is one. A person does not have both a good will and a bad will, as is commonly thought.[8] A person's will can be **directed** towards good or towards bad, but it itself is one. Thus when the will is restricted, all of its aspects are restricted at the same time.

When someone is involved in t'shuva, he has to be careful to separate both the good from the bad, and the bad from the good. He has to wield the scalpel of t'shuva like a fine surgeon who removes the malignancy without removing any healthy tissue. Moreover, he has to identify the good which has become imbedded in the bad, and to strengthen it to the same extent that he is now repelled by evil. In this manner, by rescuing his

---

8. Here, we are speaking about the will, and not about a person's inclination, or *yetzer*, which is divided between the good inclination and the bad inclination, a *yetzer hatov* and a *yetzer harah*.

longing for goodness from its dungeon of sin, his t'shuva will actually transform his former transgressions into virtues.[9]

SINS INTO VIRTUES

Rabbi Kook describes this first stage "engine shutdown" as a low level of t'shuva, in that it weakens a person's will and inhibits his character. But the lethargy, apparent depression, and lack of vitality which are caused by the fear of sin, soon are replaced by active, positive forces when a person enters the next phase of t'shuva.

"There is a shortcoming in the lower t'shuva, in that it weakens a person's will and inhibits his character. However, this shortcoming is corrected when the thought of t'shuva reaches maturity, and it is united with the exalted t'shuva which comes, not to weaken the will and to break a person's character, but rather to strengthen his will and the value of his personality. In this manner, his sins are transformed into merit, *When the wicked man turns from his wickedness, and does what is lawful and right, he shall live in those things.*"[10]

When the *baal t'shuva* feels more secure with his purer lifestyle, he begins to release his will and direct it toward the good. Reconnected to the force of goodness which powers the universe, his spirit and personality are bolstered. Like a starship put into "warp-drive," he seems to accelerate into a whole new dimension of space. The brazenness, or *chutzpah*, that he once

9.   *Orot HaT'shuva*, 9:5.
10. Ezekiel, 33:19. *Orot HaT'shuva*, 9:7.

had for sin[11] is transformed into a brazenness for holiness. We can understand the great power involved in this transformation when we recognize that sinning, which is going against G-d's will for the world, demands a lot of *chutzpah*. In this higher level of t'shuva, when a person frees his willpower from sin, by rejecting the sin and **preserving** the willpower, he uses the same high-powered *chutzpah* to form a bolder connection with G-d. He heads full blast for holiness, not settling for anything else, letting nothing stand in his way, smashing through all barriers, obstacles, and resistance. His boldness propels him to ever-new levels. This is one of the ways how sin itself helps a person do t'shuva. The willpower which previously led him to sin, is now used to worship G-d. Because he harnesses this extra "sin power" to reach Divine cleaving, he can reach greater heights than if he hadn't sinned at all.

11. This is called *azut d'kiddusha* in *Hasidut:* Rabbi Nachman of Breslov, *Likkutei Etzot, Azut* 1; *Kedushat HaLevi, Parshat Beshalach.*

135

Chapter Fourteen

T'SHUVA AND TORAH

We will learn in subsequent chapters that the national t'shuva of the Jewish people is inspired by the nation's return to the Land of Israel, and to our national spiritual treasure, the Torah. In this chapter, we shall focus, not on the comprehensive t'shuva of the nation, but rather on the symbiotic relationship between an individual's t'shuva and Torah.

YOU CAN'T HAVE ONE WITHOUT THE OTHER

First, we must understand that Torah is not external, factual knowledge like the knowledge of science, mathematics, or linguistics. Torah is an inwardly-directed knowledge which has the power to influence and change a person, to refine a person's sensitivities and to connect him to the holy, spiritual foundations of life. The study of Torah is not a quantitative amassing of information and theories like other knowledges. It is a qualitative experience demanding both moral and intellectual involvement, and a desire to make Torah ideals an essential part of one's character. When a person learns Torah and discovers the exalted harmony and goodness of Creation, his will is affected, stimulating yearnings for G-d. Because his will for goodness is enhanced, his desire for t'shuva is strengthened as well.[1]

The Talmud teaches that G-d created the evil inclination and the Torah as its cure.[2] Rabbi Kook explains this as meaning that the will cannot be perfected except through the purifying influence of the Torah.[3] The Torah strengthens the will and directs it towards holiness.

The more an individual learns Torah, especially the deeper wisdom of Torah, the more knowledgeable he becomes about his true spiritual nature and about the nature of his will. He comes to recognize that the entire world is Divinely inspired to attain a purer connection to G-d. This higher contemplation brings him to a higher level of t'shuva.

"True, complete t'shuva demands lofty horizons of perception, in order to be raised to the resplendent world which abounds in holiness and truth. This can only be done by being immersed in the secrets of life found in Divine wisdom and the depths of the Torah. This necessitates physical cleansing and the purification of one's traits as aids, so that the clouds of lust will not darken the intellect's clarity. But the study of Torah must precede everything else, especially the study of the higher, su-

1. *Orot HaTorah*, 6:1, by Rabbi Kook, Mosad HaRav Kook Publishers, Jerusalem.
2. *Kiddushin* 30B.
3. *Musar Avicha, Midot, Ratzon.*

pernal Torah, for it alone can shatter all of the iron barriers which separate the individual and the community from G-d."[4]

T'shuva and Torah go hand-in-hand. Like bees and honey, you can't have one without the other. **The more a person studies Torah, the more inspired he is to do t'shuva.**[5] **Similarly, to the extent that a person purifies himself through t'shuva, his study of Torah is blessed and made more clear.**[6]

A person who is satisfied with a routine performance of the Torah's commandments can get by with a minimum of t'shuva, but to enter into the deep, secret wellsprings of Torah, a person must be pure of all unholy influences. To reach this state of cleanliness, a great deal of t'shuva is required. The depth of a person's t'shuva enables him to understand greater degrees of Torah, for the ability to understand Torah does not solely depend on one's intellectual skills in clinically analyzing a passage of Talmud — the essence of Torah is when the person has internalized its profound moral concepts into his being, so much so that he yearns for them with all of his might. Only when a person has reached this level, when his will is so refined that it longs only for goodness, can he properly understand the deep secrets of Torah.[7] For this reason, people who profess to learn Kaballah without doing t'shuva are not really learning at all. They study the formulas of mysticism, but the import of the

4.   *Orot HaT'shuva*, 10:1.
5.   *Orot HaTorah*, 6:13.
6.   Ibid, 6:5.
7.   "The power of the will and its illumination, and intellectual prowess are interconnected, the one to the other." *Orot HaT'shuva*, 10:4. See also, 10:5 and 10:8.

teachings does not enter their hearts, for G-d only unravels the secrets of Torah to one who has prepared his soul to receive them.

"It is obvious that it is impossible to learn the secrets of Torah without t'shuva. For in these great matters, the will and the intellect are united. When one understands these subjects with a mighty will for the good, one yearns for them and devises many general and specific strategies to obtain them. However, when sins form a barrier, the will is damaged, and since one cannot rise to the highest, innermost level of the will...wisdom cannot grow in him, and the channels of understanding the secrets of Torah are blocked."[8]

Simply put, if you want to understand the inner workings of existence, you have to clean up your act. Just like you cannot purify yourself in a ritual bath while holding on to a dead mouse,[9] you cannot learn the secrets of Torah while you are living in sin.

Recently, the media has reported a boom in the learning of Kaballah. Movie stars in Hollywood, stockbrokers on Wall Street, and students in college are flocking to Kaballah clubs. While the efficacy of this learning is questionable so long as the would-be mystics remain ensconced in their usual lifestyles, the reason behind their spiritual searching is important to note:

"Therefore, in the last generations, in which the darkness of lust has so greatly increased, and the strength of the body has

8.   *Orot HaT'shuva*, 10:8.
9.   *Taanit* 16A. Rambam, *Laws of T'shuva*, 2:3.

weakened, until it is impossible to stand firm against the material onslaught, it is imperative to illuminate the darkness with the mystical secrets of Torah, which know no boundaries, and which elevate (seekers) on wings of lofty freedom to the highest ascents, and which spread the transcendental joy of the beauty of holiness to depressed and spiritually darkened souls."[10]

THE SECRET OF THE SECRETS

When speaking about the secrets of Torah, Rabbi Kook is not suggesting that everyone learn the Kaballistic formulas found in layman's books on Kaballah. He is not talking about learning the mystical meanings of the *sefirot*, the divine emanations, nor about *yichudim*, and the like. While all of these matters are required learning for those special Torah scholars who have reached states of extraordinary purity, we normal people are to focus on how these formulas appear in the world, in the life of the individual, and in the life of the nation of Israel as it rises out of exile to redemption. In effect, Rabbi Kook's writings illuminate the deeper understandings of the Torah as they are manifesting themselves today, without employing the technical language of the Kaballah, with all of its metaphors and abstractions.

JOE THE STOCKBROKER

We have mentioned that a person who desires to learn Torah without the willingness to abandon a life of sin will not benefit by the Torah's healing power. In the light of Rabbi

---

10. *Orot HaKodesh,* Rabbi Kook, Part 1, pg. 92, Mosad HaRav Kook Publishers.

Kook's teachings, let's follow a young stockbroker, Joe, to a class in Jewish mysticism, and see what is taking place in his soul.

First of all, though Joe might have been a top student at Princeton, his intellectual faculty has been distorted by sin. He may be a whiz in math, but his moral intelligence is dull. Because of the essential unity of existence, his spiritual darkness also darkens the light of the mind. On the most basic level, he does not know the difference between right and wrong. Sure, he knows that murder is evil, but other sins, including serious transgressions like stealing and adultery, do not seem so bad. In many instances, moral wrongdoings do not seem like sins at all.[11]

Rabbi Kook explains that the dulling of Joe's intelligence is due, not only to his own sins, but to the polluted and errant values of the society to which he belongs. These distorted mores are caused by the general sins of the community. Though the word of G-d is always present, in Torah, in religion, in tradition, and in the exquisite orderings of heaven and earth, the immoral norms of society act as a barrier, blocking the Heavenly light. Because Joe has become detached from Divine ideals as a result of his sins and the sins of society, he has become prey to the darker forces of life and to his weaker self. He lacks the moral fortitude to hold himself back from sin. It is only through the purification of t'shuva that his will for goodness can be strengthened and his clarity of thought restored.[12]

11. *Orot HaT'shuva*, 10:5.
12. Ibid.

When Joe attends a class in Torah and confronts its sparkling light, if he is a true seeker who truly desires a higher enlightenment, he will sense his inner darkness and reach out for
the deliverance that only t'shuva can bring. Though there be
wrongdoings which he cannot address at the moment, whether
through spiritual weakness or practical impediments, the Torah
that he continues to learn will bring clarity to his thinking and
fortify his will, providing him with the moral resolve which he
lacks.[13]

As he elevates himself to a higher perception of life, his
sins will rise up before him to hold back his t'shuva. For instance, if he committed adultery with a married woman, he may
ask himself how can he ever confess his wrongdoing and face
up to his wife, and to the betrayed husband. If he fails to redress this transgression, it will stand in his way like a wall,
blocking out the spiritual light for which he longs. To the extent
that he puts his t'shuva into action, his thoughts will be
straightened, his perceptions blessed, and his life will be filled
with joy.[14]

If Joe has read Rabbi Kook writings on t'shuva, he has a
sign letting him know if his path of t'shuva is on the right
track. If he feels a joy in the learning of Torah, if he is able to
clearly grasp its deep, mystical concepts, then his t'shuva is real.[15]
With each sin that is corrected, additional vistas of learning open
before him.[16] The most supreme enlightenment comes when he

13. Ibid, 10:6 and 9.
14. Ibid, 10:7.
15. Ibid, 10:2, 2a.
16. Ibid, 10:3.

realizes in all of his being that cleaving to G-d is the greatest joy in life.[17] Reaching this level, he will experience a profound humbleness, for, "How can any person feel an egotistical pride when he stands before the Source of all perfection, before the infinite light that transcends all blessings and praises?"[18]

When Joe, the stockbroker, realizes that t'shuva makes the world go round, and not the New York Stock Exchange, he has truly become a *baal t'shuva*.

PRAYER FROM THE HEART

It is impossible to speak about the relationship between t'shuva and Torah without mentioning the vital importance of prayer. Often, in the light of the Torah, when confronted by one's wrongdoings and moral impurity, one longs for a far-reaching t'shuva which is clearly beyond one's immediate grasp. At times, this great leap forward cannot be actualized until it is accompanied by heartfelt prayer. It is prayer which opens the stream of Divine assistance which is needed to overcome weakness and fear, hurdle over chasms of darkness, and redress every transgression of the past, so that ever-new perceptions can be grasped.[19] King David was a master of t'shuva[20] and a master of prayer.[21] To this day, his Psalms are our ladders to G-d.

---

17. Ibid, 10:4.
18. Ibid.
19. Ibid, 10:10 and 11.
20. *Moed Katan* 16B. *Avodah Zara* 5A.
21. Psalms, 6:10; 28:6; 103:1; 120:1; 130:2; 142:1-2; 145:8.

To summarize, the more you learn Torah, the more t'shuva you will be inspired to do — and the more t'shuva you do, the more Torah you are able to learn.

Chapter Fifteen

BARRIERS TO T'SHUVA

"TURN BACK FROM YOUR SINS!"

After analyzing the many different facets of t'shuva, Rabbi Kook explains what happens to a person who sets out on a path of return. The first thing we should know is that there are many barriers to t'shuva.[1] To begin with, when someone is not accustomed to sounds of holiness, his ears are blocked to t'shuva's constant call.[2]

Life's inner moral demand calls out to man, "Turn back from your sins!"[3] Sometimes this inner moral compunction begins as a soft echo barely audible in the conscience. Was it a voice? Did I hear someone calling? Little by little, it gains in

---

1.   Rambam, *Laws of T'shuva*, Chapter Four.
2.   *Avot*, 6:2. *Kedushat HaLevi, Parshat Shlach*.
3.   *Orot HaT'shuva*, 13:8.

volume and insistency until it thunders, SON OF MAN, RE-TURN FROM YOUR EVIL WAYS!

Occasionally this voice calls out so loudly, it rings in a person's ear wherever he goes. It won't give him rest. "RETURN!" it calls out in the discoteque. "RETURN!" it calls out at the beach.

"Leave me alone!" the hounded soul cries out. No longer can he pretend not to listen. No longer can he remain in the chains of crass material existence with all of its vices and pulls.

At this point, Rabbi Kook says, a person must rise to a higher spiritual level in order to find inner peace. He must summon inner courage to face this spiritual crisis. Sometimes, however, the moral demands of t'shuva seem so great, a person despairs of ever being able to escape the clutches of sin. His transgressions, like thorns, pin him down on every side. Outside forces seem to control him. He sees no possible way of making amends.

Once again, Rabbi Kook offers hope by telling us that it is precisely from this point of despair that G-d's mercy will shine.[4] *A broken and contrite heart, O G-d, Thou will not despise.*[5]

WHERE THERE IS A WILL, THERE IS A WAY

Sometimes when a person has a passionate desire to do t'shuva, he longs to perfect everything all at once. Discovering

4.   Ibid.
5.   Psalms, 51:19.

a world of greater morality, he immediately wants to actualize it in life. A sudden spiritual illumination has raised him out of his darkness, and he wants all of his actions, thoughts, and character traits to be immediately on the same holy level. With all that needs to be corrected, he does not know where to begin. It is easier to contemplate a state of absolute morality than to achieve it in everyday life. The more t'shuva he does, the more he feels the gap between where he is and where he should be. Without a firm foundation in the realm of the holy, he can easily grow discouraged and lose his resolve to become a more moral person. As a result, people who begin learning about Judaism, and about their inner spiritual world, often put on the brakes in fear of experiencing further letdown in not being able to reach their ideals.

"If a person wants all of his inner sensitivities and powers to be instantly renewed in line with the spiritual elevation which he has discovered, and expects all of his immoral ways to be immediately straightened and perfected — he will lack inner stability, and he will not be able to fortify his will to follow the path to true perfection."[6]

The solution, Rabbi Kook says, is to do t'shuva in stages. First of all, one should console oneself with the knowledge that the very thought of t'shuva, the very desire to perfect the wrongs of one's life, is t'shuva itself.[7] This very understanding brings great inner correction in its wake. With this recognition, a person can feel more relaxed, feeling certain that the t'shuva process is already underway.

6.   *Orot HaT'shuva*, 13:6. See also, 13:10.
7.   See Chapter Eight of this book.

Next, a person must intensify the illumination of holiness within him. This is to be found in the study of Torah. As we have learned, the study of Torah strengthens the will to do t'shuva and refines character traits and modes of behavior.[8]

After the will for t'shuva has been firmly established, the person is ready for the details of t'shuva. This stage has two aspects: t'shuva over behavior in the future, and t'shuva over transgressions in the past.[9] Once again, the Torah provides the guidance and light. The Torah translates the ideal moral standards which the person has discovered into the details of day-to-day living.[10]

FOCUS ON THE FUTURE

"The foundation of t'shuva should always be established on the goal of improving the future. In the beginning of the t'shuva process, correcting the past should not be seen as an impeding prerequisite. If a person would immediately start by redressing the past, he would encounter many obstacles, and the paths of t'shuva, and the coming closer to G-d, would seem to be too difficult. However, if a person truly endeavors to refine his future deeds, Divine assistance is promised, even in correcting transgressions of the past."[9]

Since it is easier to commit oneself to a more positive life in the future, this is the place to start. For instance, a person decides that from now on he will not say anything bad about

8.   See Chapter Fourteen of this book.
9.   *Orot HaT'shuva*, 13:9b.
10. Ibid, 13:5a.

people. This future-oriented t'shuva is easier to pinpoint and work on. Someone can even make a list of goals and refer to it every day to help him keep on his course. This way, consistent progress will be made and feelings of frustration will become less and less acute.

It is much harder to figure out how you are going to mend wrongdoings which you have done in the past. First of all, a person may not remember all of his sins. For example, it is hard to remember all of the bad things one might have said about people. It is even harder to remember to whom they were said. How can a person find everyone in order to make amends? A situation like this can cause a person to give up in despair.

Rabbi Kook's advice is to set out correcting the transgressions of the past which are within the person's reach to correct. This will set into motion a snowball of t'shuva whose inner force will lead him to correct matters more and more difficult, until he succeeds in redressing all wrongs.[11]

In summary, stage one is the consolation in knowing that the thought of t'shuva is already t'shuva. Stage two is developing a firmer base in the Torah. Stage three is the resolve not to sin in the future. Stage four, the resolve to gradually address the wrongs of the past, beginning with the matters that are easiest to mend.

NITTY GRITTY T'SHUVA

Ironically, the commandments of the Torah, the very path-

11. Ibid, 13:6.

ways to freedom, are often seen as barriers to t'shuva. People who are seeking horizons of ideal justice and universal peace can feel constricted by the Torah's demands. They feel frustrated by the nitty-gritty details of the law. They erroneously believe that t'shuva is a retreat from the world, a journey toward spiritual isolation and pure contemplation, away from the complex moral dilemmas of everyday life. These people maintain that since the world is corrupt, and since they yearn to be moral, they will avoid all contact with worldly matters. Thus, the commandments of the Torah, with their focus on perfecting practical life, are seen as barriers to their goals.

We have mentioned that a strategy of worldly separation may be a helpful early phase of t'shuva, but it is not the end of the journey. In fact it ends in spiritual limbo, leaving a person isolated on a mountaintop, neither in heaven, nor down on earth. Rabbi Kook writes that there is a far superior strategy. This is the study of the *Choshen Mishpat*, the civil laws which govern man's dealings with his fellow man, laws involving money, property, contracts and the like.[12] A Jew should become versed in all of its details in order to know precisely the principles of Divine justice on earth. For instance, Rabbi Kook writes:

"It is especially important to do t'shuva regarding transgressions against other people, especially regarding theft, which hinders the elevation of the will. A person must be stringent in this and trust in G-d's assistance to attain the state of purity

---

12. *Choshen Mishpat* comprises the largest tract of the *Shulchan Aruch*, the code of Jewish law.

where he will reject anything associated with unjust gain and oppression."[13]

Learning the laws of the *Hoshen Mishpat* will guard a person from uncertainty and error, and offer clear guidelines in the day-to-day dealings of life. In addition to this study, and to the regular study of the Torah's many branches, Rabbi Kook teaches that special attention must be given to heightening moral sensitivities, and to the contemplation of exalted spiritual concepts, so that the soul will long for Divine justice in every aspect of life. This will bring the light of t'shuva to all facets of social interaction.[14] In this manner, a person not only betters himself, he also improves the world.

Thus, it is not the Torah which is a barrier to t'shuva, but rather the false ideas which people have about spirituality. Spirituality is not something intended for monasteries and isolated mountain peaks, but for everyday life in society, in the supermarket, in the bank, in the courtroom, and in the house. The t'shuva ideal is not to turn into a monk. One isn't to say, because I am influenced by people, I will avoid them; because I am influenced by food, I will not eat; because I am influenced by women, I will be celibate.[15] One isn't to reject life, but to uplift it. Our task is to hallow even the nitty-gritty details of day-to-day existence. It is easy to turn one's back on life, to walk out the door, to stick out your tongue at your past and say, "Goodbye world, I'm headed off for the mountains!" The higher t'shuva is down-to-earth t'shuva; deed by deed, person

13.   *Orot HaT'shuva*, 8:14.
14.   *Orot HaT'shuva*, 13:5 and 5a.
15.   Rambam, *Laws of T'shuva*, 3:11.

by person, food by food. T'shuva comes to sanctify life, not to abandon it to despair.

THE SHOW MUST GO ON

Even if a person feels that transgressions from his past are blocking his will to repent, Rabbi Kook says the show must go on — t'shuva must go forward.[16] **T'shuva must never stop. T'shuva has no end. Life must be filled with t'shuva.**

Occasionally, the thought of mending each and every sin is just too overwhelming for a person to deal with. Who has the energy? Who has the strength? Who can muster the humility it takes to apologize to everyone he has slighted? The magnitude of the endeavor before him can even lead a person to say, why bother, t'shuva won't help.

Let no weakness stand in the way. T'shuva must continue. It must overcome all obstacles. Even if there are matters which seem impossible to correct, let a man always find joy in every bit of t'shuva that comes to his grasp. The merit of fixing the things that he can will stand by him, helping him to overcome more difficult barriers. Finally, Rabbi Kook assures us, with G-d's help, he will be able to mend all that needs to be mended.[17]

BARRIERS OF SIN

Millions of people all over the world are searching for a

16.   *Orot HaT'shuva*, 13:5 and 5a.
17.   Ibid, 13:9 and 9a.

deeper understanding and connection to G-d. What makes finding Him so difficult? Why is it so hard to fathom the depths of Divinity? Rabbi Kook explains that the difficulties are due to people's sins and unrefined traits, which weaken a person's will for perfection and goodness.

"In order to remove every barrier between the general Divine good and the individual who yearns for it, it is necessary to separate oneself from every moral blemish, in the widest sense, including the cleansing of all of one's character traits and the purifying of intellectual endeavors, for it is through these that G-d's light appears in the world...."[18]

Bad character attributes, whether they be jealousy, anger, cynicism, pride, stinginess, laziness, and the like, together with whatever sins a person might have, all block his connection to G-d. They darken the intellect with spiritual pollution, and clog the channels of holiness which connect this world with the Divine. If a person feels that a closeness to G-d is eluding him, though he try and try to please Him, self-introspection is needed to discover what negative traits and sins are preventing further progress.

In the initial phase of t'shuva, we focus our microscopes on our general behavior, without turning up the light. We have to deal with the glaring wrongdoings first, before we can begin to see which fine tunings are still in need of adjustment. Then, as we become more sensitive to the holy and spiritual, we have to do t'shuva on our original t'shuva. **The more we purify our-**

18.   Ibid, 13:2.

selves, the clearer our moral and spiritual vision becomes, and we discover that there is still plenty more t'shuva to do.[19]

TAMING THE BEAST

Sometimes, in a person's longing to cleanse himself completely, he may decide that since his sins stem from his material yearnings, he will wage war on his physical life and become an ascetic who barely eats. This person's intentions are certainly praiseworthy. His passionate desire for inspiration and connection to G-d is noble, but in letting his longings push him to starve his body, he is in fact sinning against himself.[20]

Precisely because t'shuva is the most exciting sensation in the world, a person must be careful to control the great powers it unleashes. **The turned-on t'shuva "junkie" who wakes up in the morning looking to shoot holiness into his veins is faced with a problem. He wants too much, too fast.** If in his frustration, he blames his body and its lusts, he can start to wage war on himself. He tries to uproot all of his feelings and passions, including healthy drives like eating and sleeping. But the body resists. It still wants to eat, to sleep, to have normal, marital relations. As long as a person continues to breathe, the monster called the body will not go away.

When this aggressive strategy fails, the person can fall into despair. His longing to fly straight up to heaven has been thwarted. Instead of feeling rejected, however, he should realize that the body and soul need to rise up the spiritual ladder to-

19. *Mesillat Yesharim*, Chapter 3.
20. *Nazir* 3A.

gether. Patience is needed. With all of his spiritual and physical baggage, he sets out on the trip. Little by little, he will prod the beast, poke here and there, steering it, training it, making it obey his commands.

A person comes to learn that as sensual and materialistic as one's body can be, it also has rights. Just as it is forbidden to hurt another person, it is forbidden to hurt oneself.[21] Just as one has to be kind to others, one has to be kind to oneself.[22] A baal t'shuva who accepts upon himself extra stringencies has to take counsel with himself to know when the border has been crossed.

For instance, a person may feel that fasting can help him weaken his material lusts. Not wanting to exhaust himself completely, he may decide that instead of fasting a whole day, it is healthier to fast during the day, but to eat at night. In this manner, a person may learn to rule over his lusts without draining his body and willpower completely. If this regimen also proves too punishing, then the person must have compassion on himself and try to find another strategy to cleanse himself of his lusts.[23]

G-D TO THE RESCUE

The main thing is not to despair. As long as a person's will remains firm, G-d will help him on his way. He must come to recognize that the ultimate solution to his problems does not rest

21. Rambam, *Laws of Damages*, 5:1.
22. *Vayikra Rabbah*, 34:3.
23. *Orot HaT'shuva*, 13:7.

with himself, for a person by himself cannot correct all of his failings. He has to know that in the end, the charity of G-d, His mercy and lofty salvation will rescue him from his darkness.[24] G-d will answer his yearnings and bring him to the higher deliverance for which he so longs.[25]

THE ART OF T'SHUVA

Rabbi Kook adds one final point which is important to stress. Many people reject the idea of t'shuva because they believe that they will have to give up their personalities, talents, and uniqueness in order to conform to a rigid religious standard. Rabbi Kook says that just the opposite is needed. The *baal t'shuva* must follow his own special path, not someone else's. Without fear, he must expand his unique intellectual and imaginative talents in the freedom of his soul, in line with his own individuality. T'shuva does not restrict life — it enhances it. The musician need not give up his music; the writer need not abandon his pen; the singer need not refrain from singing; the businessman need not give up his business. The opposite is true. The *baal t'shuva* must use his talents, without hesitation or fear, in serving G-d, in declaring His praises, in bringing the joy and knowledge of G-d to the world. Then his t'shuva will be complete. Not only in mending his deeds and improving his ways, but by sanctifying his unique individuality and talents to G-d, he helps bring the whole world to completion.[26]

24. *Kiddushin* 30B.
25. Ibid.
26. Ibid, 13:10.

Chapter Sixteen

ISRAEL AND THE WORLD

FIRST IN T'SHUVA

We have learned that the force of t'shuva is perpetually at work, propelling all of life toward perfection. While the enlightenment of mankind is a gradually developing process, the day is soon coming when the wonder of t'shuva will capture all imaginations and hearts.

In this saga of universal redemption, where do the Jewish people fit in? What role do they play? Just as one might expect, *Am Yisrael* is to be the leader, blazing the trail for all other peoples to follow.

"The Jewish people, because of their enhanced spiritual nature, will be the first nation in the world to do t'shuva. The special spirit of t'shuva will initially be revealed in this portion of humanity. Israel is propelled from within to be united with G-d's light in the world, which is free of transgression and wrongdoing. Every falling away (from its connection to G-d) blemishes the wholeness of its inner perfection, yet in the end, its powerful life-force will triumph over the deviation, and it will return to complete health. This complete health will start to invigorate (the nation) with great strength and the light of t'shuva will shine within her first. Afterward, Israel will be the special channel to spread life's inner yearning for t'shuva to all of the world, to lighten the world's darkness and elevate its stature."[1]

As we mentioned in Chapter Six, Israel's enhanced spiritual nature lies in its unique holiness and connection to G-d.

For thou art a holy people to the L-rd thy G-d; the L-rd thy G-d has chosen thee to be a special people to Himself, above all people that are upon the face of the earth."[2]

The nation of Israel has an exalted inner content which radiates G-d's blessing to the world.[3] This *segula*, or unique Divine connection, encompasses all of the Jewish people. It is our national soul. Blemishes caused by sin are always external to the soul of the nation, leaving no permanent scar.[4]

1. *Orot HaT'shuva*, 5:8. *Orot, Orot HaTechiya*, 72. See Judges 13:24.
2. Deut. 7:6.
3. *Kuzari*, 2:36; *Orot*, pg. 138.
4. Maharal, *Netzach Yisrael*, Chapter Eleven. In his book *Orot*, Rabbi Kook writes: "The nation of Israel has an eternal covenant that it will never become completely impure. Impurity can influence it; it can darken the nation with blemishes, but it cannot uproot the nation from its source of Divine life. Many of the adherents to the (national pioneering) spirit of the nation which has presently awakened, claim that they do not

Israel's deep, inner yearning to be connected to G-d, triumphs in the end, banishing all darkness. We are not speaking about a spiritual awakening of scattered individuals. THE WHOLE NATION RETURNS TO G-D. True to the prophecy of Moses, the whole nation will return to live by the Torah.[5] Politicians and soldiers, artists and farmers, teachers and judges will have one common purpose — to sanctify life's every endeavor. Israel will return to being itself — *A kingdom of priests and a holy nation.*[6]

The revelation of Israel's holiness will bring more light to the world than the sun.[7] Mankind will be blinded and stunned. All people will proclaim:

Surely this great nation is a wise and understanding people. For what nation is so great that has G-d so near to them... and what nation is so great that has statutes and judgments so righteous as all of this Torah?[8]

This awakened, holy nation will demand a new life order, the correction of all wrong, the uprooting of all evil, rescue for

need a connection to the Spirit of G-d in rebuilding the nation... but they themselves do not know what it is that they seek, for the spirit of the Israeli nation is so deeply connected to the Spirit of G-d which infuses the life of the nation, that even a person who says that he has no need for G-d's spirit is himself attached to it, in spite of what he says, because of his yearning to be a part of the Jewish nation." *Orot*, pg. 63.

5.   Deut., 30:8.
6.   Exodus, 19:6.
7.   Isaiah, 24:23.
8.   Deut., 4:6-8.

the downtrodden, equality for all people, food for all children, salvation from a life of paganism and sin.

Inspired by the holy nation of Israel, mankind will abandon its vain and misguided paths, and a mighty spirit of t'shuva will be ignited throughout the world. Nations will flock to Israel to learn the ways of the Jews.

And it shall come to pass in the last days, that the mountain of the L-rd's House shall be established on the top of the mountains, and shall be exalted above the hills; and all the nations shall flow unto it. And many people shall go and say, Come, let us go up to the mountain of the L-rd, to the House of the G-d of Yaacov; and He will teach us His ways, and we will walk in His paths, for out of Zion shall go forth Torah, and the word of the L-rd from Jerusalem.[9]

AN END TO WORLD DARKNESS

An example of Israel's future influence on the nations will help make this utopian scenario more clear. Rabbi Kook writes that t'shuva is ever-present in the inner fabric of existence because it was brought into being before the creation of the world. Before sin had occurred, a remedy for it had already been prepared.[10]

This understanding is in dramatic contrast to Christianity's doctrine of original sin. From a Christian point of view, man, by definition, is a sinner. He is damned from birth, born into purgatory, and can only be saved in the life to come. This teach-

---

9. Isaiah, 2:2-4.
10. *Orot HaT'shuva*, 6:2. See *Pesachim* 54A.

ing dooms mankind from the start and lays the foundation for the moral decadence and corruption rampant throughout the Christian world. Just as a gloom and darkness fills Christianity's famous cathedrals and Notre Dames, the doctrine of original sin has hung a suffocating cloud of guilt and repression over human existence.[11]

In contrast, Judaism teaches that original sin is not original. T'shuva came first. Before sin appeared in the world, a remedy had already been prepared. This means that a man is born, not into a prison of sin, but into a condition of t'shuva, into a world of hope, of improvement, and progress. Man is not doomed to despair. Should he fall, t'shuva is there to raise him and to restore his connection to G-d.

This is one of the lights that Israel will bring to the nations.[12] The light of t'shuva. The example of Israel will offer hope for the world, salvation from Christian doctrines of purgatory, and a truly, purifying, living connection to G-d **here on earth.**

We have learned that the t'shuva of the Jewish people is certain. Furthermore, it is the t'shuva of Israel which will lead the world to universal perfection. But how will this great t'shuva come about? What causes the scattered, exiled Jewish nation to return to the glorious days of our past?[13] Rabbi Kook cites two interrelated paths: first, the nation's return to the Land of Israel, and secondly, our mass return to Torah.

11. See, *War and Peace*, Chapter Five.
12. Isaiah, 42:6; 49:6; 51:4.
13. Lamentations, 5:21. Prayer on returning the Torah scroll to the ark.

Chapter Seventeen

ERETZ YISRAEL

We have learned that t'shuva encompasses far more than personal repentance. Its ever-streaming waves effect the world in its entirety, lifting it toward perfection. Furthermore, we have learned that it is the nation of Israel who will lead the world to redemption, marching in front of the parade of nations with its shofars blaring away.

This is all well and good. But what will bring the Jewish people to t'shuva? What will awaken the Divine voice in its soul? What causes the scattered, exiled Jewish nation to return, as we beseech G-d in our prayers, to the glorious days of our past?[1]

Rabbi Kook writes that the rebirth of the Jewish nation

---

1.   Lamentations, 5:21.

in *Eretz Yisrael* is the foundation for the ultimate t'shuva, both for the nation of Israel, and for the whole world.[2]

THE HOLY LAND

To understand this concept fully, one must understand the incomparable holiness of *Eretz Yisrael* and its importance to the nation of Israel. While it is beyond the scope of this book to explore this subject in depth,[3] we will mention a few of the things which point to the unique connection between the Jewish people and their Land.

The Jewish people possess true national vitality only in the Land of Israel.[4] Outside of the Land, Jews can excel as individuals in all fields of endeavor; there can be great Torah scholars, but the light of G-d cannot appear in a national format. Only in the Land of Israel can the Jews be a *KINGDOM of priests and a holy NATION*.[5] The *Zohar* emphasizes that the Jews can be a nation only in Israel, and not outside of it.[6] Prophecies of redemption all involve the return of the Jewish people to the Land of Israel and the restoration of Jewish sovereignty over the

2.   *Orot HaT'shuva*, 17:1.
3.   Readers interested in exploring this subject further are encouraged to study Rabbi Kook's book, *Orot*, Chapter One, *Eretz Yisrael*; and see the English commentary, *Lights on Orot*, by Rabbi David Samson and Tzvi Fishman, Torat Eretz Yisrael Publications. See also, *Torat Eretz Yisrael*, Chapters 3-15, Rabbi David Samson, Torat Eretz Yisrael Publications.
4.   Isaiah, 42:5.
5.   Exodus, 19:6.
6.   *Zohar, Vayikra* 93B.

Land.[7] The Jewish people's unique prophetic talent is dependent on being in the Land of Israel.[8] The Temple can only be rebuilt on *Har HaBayit*, and the full revelation of G-d's Presence is exclusive to *Eretz Yisrael*, as the prophet teaches, *For Torah will go forth from Zion, and the word of the L-rd from Jerusalem.*[9]

In a letter, Rabbi Kook writes:

"The source of the moral baseness which continues to darken the world stems from the lack of recognition regarding the value and wisdom of the Land of Israel. Thus the sin of the Spies,[10] who spoke derogatorily about the pleasant Land, remains uncorrected. To rectify this, the Land's praise, splendor, holiness, and honor must be declared to all of the world."[11]

While Rabbi Kook emphasizes that the t'shuva of the Jewish people and a return to the Torah go hand-in-hand,[12] he indicates that a preliminary stage of national revival will bring this spiritual awakening to pass. First, the Jewish people must return to Zion to rebuild their homeland. Once the physical body that houses the nation is built, then the revitalized Jewish

---

7.   Ezekiel, 37:21-22.
8.   *Moed Kattan* 25A; *Kuzari*, 1:95, 2:8-24.
9.   Isaiah, 2:3.
10. The reference is to the Spies whom Moshe sent to reconnoiter the Land of Israel after the Jews left Egypt. Their negative report discouraged the nation from entering the Land, and the generation was punished with death in the Wilderness. Numbers, 13:1-25; Deut., 1:21-39.
11. Letters, Vol. 1, pgs. 112-113.
12. See Chapter Eighteen of this book.

soul will yearn for spiritual completion as well, and our people will flock back to the Torah.

HOMEWARD BOUND

We shall try to explain this in a simple manner. We have mentioned that the concept of t'shuva means to return. Suppose a man is expelled from his house by thieves. The wrongdoing will only be corrected when the owner returns to repossess his house.

For the world to reach perfection, G-d decreed that the Jewish people must live a life of Torah in Israel. G-d's first commandment to Abraham is to go to the Land of Israel in order to serve G-d in the most complete way.[13] Afterwards G-d commands Moshe to bring the Jews out from Egypt to *Eretz Yisrael.* Over and over, the Torah repeats that the Jewish people are to live their unique Torah life in Israel.[14] **When the holy Jewish nation lives a holy life of Torah in the Holy Land, the vessel is formed to bring the light of G-d to the world.** The nation of Israel becomes an international beacon, an example and light to all of the nations in the world.[15]

At the time of the Second Temple, when we failed to uphold the high moral standard demanded of us by the Torah, we were punished and exiled from the Land. G-d's worldly vessel was shattered. Israel was conquered, Jerusalem was razed, the Land was laid waste. G-d's chosen people were scattered and

13. *Genesis,* 12:1. Also *Kuzari,* 2:14.
14. Deut. 1:8, 1:26, 3:18, 4:1, 4:5, 4:14, 5:27-30, 6:1-3, 6:18, 7:13, 8:1, 11:1...
15. Isaiah, 42:6.

debased. Like the Jews, G-d's Presence went into exile.[16] His light in the world became hidden. In effect, mankind was cut off from G-d. Thus to rectify this tragedy and return the world to G-d, the Jewish people must return to their previous stature, including a national life in Israel, the only place in the world where the Torah can be observed in all of its wholeness because of the many commandments unique to the Land.[17]

On a deeper level, the *Zohar* teaches that the nation of Israel, Torah, and G-d are one.[18] Each Jew has a bit of the *Shekhina*, or the Presence of G-d, within him. When a Jew returns to the Land of Israel, he is, in effect, bringing G-d back with him.[19] This is the Kabbalistic concept of "raising up the buried sparks of holiness from the *klipot*."[20] Since the soul of a Jew is infused with the light of the *Shekhina*, when the Jewish people return en masse to Israel, the light of G-d in the world returns with them.

A visual illustration will help us envision what Rabbi Kook is seeing when he looks at the awakened Zionist movement. It is a global vision, spanning all human history. To raise ourselves to a more encompassing perspective, imagine being in a satellite orbiting the earth. Down below, scattered all over the globe, are tiny, little lights. These lights are the Jews, scattered

---

16. *Megillah* 29A.
17. *Sifrei, Ekev, 11:18,* Rashi, Deut., 11:18, and Ramban, Leviticus, 18:25. It is important to note that even the commandments which are not unique to the Land are performed in their fullness only in *Eretz Yisrael.*
18. *Zohar, Vayikra* 73A.
19. Rashi, Deut. 30:3.
20. *Musar Avicha, Midot HaRiyah,* pgs. 120-122. See *Innerspace,* Rabbi A. Kaplan, Moznaim Publishing Co., pg. 82.

all over the world. Slowly, lights begin to travel to a certain point on the globe — the Land of Israel. More and more lights begin to congregate there. From all over the world, the scattered lights start to unite in Israel. Lights that do not make the journey begin to flicker and disappear. Soon, a great beacon of light is formed in Israel, sending out rays of light to all of the world. These rays are the lights of t'shuva, summoning mankind back to G-d.

ZIONISM AND NATIONAL T'SHUVA

Rabbi Kook teaches that even in the return of the non-religious Zionists to Israel there is a profound holy core. The inner source of their desire to return is the Divine Ideal itself.[21] With time, it will surely be awakened. This great transformation may take fifty years. It may take one hundred. We need to remember that after nearly two-thousand years in exile, a few generations is like the blink of an eye. The important thing to know is that the t'shuva of the nation is sure to come.[22]

"The awakened yearning of the Jewish people as a whole to return to their Land, to their roots, to their spirit and way of life — truthfully, there is the light of t'shuva in this."[23]

The book of Ezekiel includes an overview of Jewish history which traces Israel's exile among the gentile nations, and her ultimate return to the Land of Israel and Torah. **Only after the nation's physical revival in Israel do the Jewish people un-**

21. *Orot, Eretz Yisrael,* 8. See *Lights on Orot,* Chapter Eight.
22. Rambam, *Laws of T'shuva,* 7:5.
23. *Orot HaT'shuva,* 17:2.

dergo the period of spiritual cleansing which leads them back to Torah.

For I will take you from among the nations, and gather you out of all countries, and I will bring you into your own land. **Then I will sprinkle pure water upon you, and you shall be clean; from all of your uncleanlinesses, and from all of your idols, will I cleanse you.** *A new heart will I also give you, and a new spirit will I put within you; and I will take away the stony heart out of your flesh, and I will give you a heart of flesh. And I will put My spirit in you, and cause you to follow My statutes, and you shall keep My judgments and do them. And you shall dwell in the land that I gave to your fathers; and you shall be My people, and I shall be your G-d.*[24]

The return to our true national identity, and the spiritual revolution which follows, encompasses all aspects of Jewish life. This great return, while still in its nascent stages, is something we have witnessed in our century. First, out of the graveyards of exile, came a new hope and zest for life, as if our scattered, dry bones were rising to rebirth.[25] Out of the ashes of the Holocaust, the Jewish nation was reborn in Israel. The Hebrew language was restored. After two-thousand years of wandering, the Jews returned to being an independent nation in their own Land. An incredible, new awakening of Jewish valor and physical prowess, epitomized by the Israel Defense Forces, startled the world. The ingathering of exiles from the four corners of the earth led to the building of a dynamic, progressive society. Yeshivas were opened all over the country. Today, Israel is un-

24. Ezekiel, 36:24-28.
25. Ezekiel, 37:1-14.

questionably the Torah center of the world. All of these things are aspects of t'shuva, of a nation returning to its roots.

As Rabbi Kook writes:

"Without question, the light of *Mashiach* and the salvation of Israel, the rebirth of the nation and the Land, the revival of its language and literature — all stem from the source of t'shuva, and out of the depths to the heights of the highest t'shuva, everything will be brought."[26]

The return of a scattered people to its Land is no simple matter. Because of the magnitude of the undertaking, there are numerous problems. Nonetheless, Rabbi Kook assures us that our inner longing for G-d will overcome all of the barriers. Even the brazen secularism, which seems so contrary to the nation's holiest goals, will become a powerful vessel bursting with Torah.

"Out of the profane, holiness will also come forth, and out of wanton freedom, the beloved yoke (of Torah) will blossom. Golden chains will be woven and arise out of secular poetry, and a brilliant light of t'shuva will shine from secular literature. This will be the supreme wonder of the vision of redemption. Let the bud sprout, let the flower blossom, let the fruit ripen, and the whole world will know that the Spirit of G-d is speaking within the nation of Israel in its every expression. All of this will climax in a t'shuva which will bring healing and redemption to the world."[27]

26. *Orot HaT'shuva*, 4:11.
27. Ibid, 17:3.

FIRST THE BODY THEN THE SPIRIT

Indeed, the revival of the Jewish people in Israel is a wonder that is impossible to explain in any mundane fashion. Clearly, there are powerful inner forces at work as we return to our homeland and slowly turn away from alien cultures and creeds. Increasingly sensitized to our own national longings, we realize that gentile lands cannot be called home. The process takes time. The nation is not transformed overnight. But gradually, the curse of *galut* is erased. From being a scattered people, the Jewish nation returns to have its own sovereign state. G-d's blessing is revealed in all facets of the nation's existence; military success, economic prosperity, scientific achievement, the resettlement of the nation's ancient cities and holy sites — all leading to a great national t'shuva, the renewal of prophecy, and, of course, the return of the Divine Presence to the rebuilt Temple in Jerusalem, in fulfillment of our prayers.[28]

Rabbi Kook explains that the secular, physical rebuilding must necessarily precede the spiritual building. The Talmud teaches that the *Beit HaMikdash* was first constructed in a normal, profane manner, and only after its completion was its sanctity declared.[29] First, Adam was created from the dust of the earth, and then the soul was placed within him.[30] So too, a Jewish youth only becomes responsible to keep the Torah at the age of thirteen after his body and mind have developed in strength. This is the pattern of spiritual building; first comes the physical

---

28. *Shemona Esrei* Prayer.
29. *Me'ilah* 14A.
30. Genesis, 2:7.

vessel, and then its inner content. First the ark is constructed, and then the Tablets are placed within.[31]

It must be remembered that the Zionist movement did not begin with Herzl, but rather with the giants of Torah, the Baal Shem Tov and the Gaon of Vilna, more than a hundred years earlier. He sent his students to settle *Eretz Yisrael*, teaching that the active resettlement of the Land was the path to bring the long-awaited redemption.[32] Other great Rabbis, Rav Tzvi Hirsh Kalisher, Rav Eliyahu Guttmacher, and Rav Shmuel Mohliver were the actual builders of the early Zionist groups like the "Lovers of Zion."[33] As the movement spread, its message attracted many non-religious Jews as well. Rabbi Kook explains that the newcomers embraced the call to Zion in a way which fit their own understandings, national aspirations, and dreams. While this temporarily lowered the loftiness of the message, it insured the necessary first stage of physical rebuilding.

"Occasionally, a concept falls from its loftiness and its original pureness after it has been grounded in life when unrefined people become associated with it, darkening its illumination. The descent is only temporary because an idea which embraces spiritual goodness cannot be transformed into evil. The descent is passing, and it is also a bridge to an approaching ascent."[34]

---

31. See Rashi, Exodus, 38:22.
32. See *Kol HaTor*, Rabbi Hillel of Shklov, on the teachings of his rabbi, the Gaon of Vilna.
33. For a detailed discussion of Rabbis involved in the Zionist movement, see *Torat Eretz Yisrael*, Chapter Nine.
34. *Orot HaT'shuva*, 12:12.

The original, pure, lofty idea of Zionism, as handed down by our Sages, is that the revival of the Jewish nation in Israel is the earthly foundation for the revelation of the Kingdom of G-d in the world.[35] For the secular Zionists, the return to Israel become something else. For some, the Land of Israel was merely a refuge from the persecutions of the gentiles. For others, it was a place to build a utopian socialist society. Because of their large numbers, the influence of the secular Zionists was widespread. Additionally, Rabbi Kook explains, the secular Jews were more suited to the task of settling the barren, swamp-ridden land. The religious Jews of the time lived in a spiritual world, having little contact with earthly matters. The physical sides of their natures were neglected and weak. The secular Jews, on the other hand, had an abundance of physical energy and prowess, along with the subsequent "will and desire to work and achieve, to carry out one's goal through physical force and concrete endeavor."[36]

When a holy idea needs to be grounded in reality, it necessarily descends from its exalted elevation. When this happens, people of lesser spiritual sensitivities seize the idea and profane its true intent. Because greater numbers of people can grasp the idea in its minimized form, its followers increase, bringing more strength and vigor to its practical implementation. This trend continues until powerful spiritual figures arise,[37] girded with the

---

35. Zohar, Ki Tisah, 276A. Rashbam, Exodus, 15:18. See *Em HaBanim Semaicha*, pgs. 57-58, Machon Pri HaAretz Publications (1983 edition).

36. *Orot HaT'shuva*, 12:13.

37. Elsewhere in *Orot HaT'shuva*, Rabbi Kook writes, "Numerous individuals may be uplifted to the ideal essence inherent in the soul of the Jewish nation through the t'shuva of one individual who is driven

strength of Divine righteousness. They grasp the idea in its original purity and hold it aloft, rescuing it from the depths where it had plunged, stripped of its holiness and spiritual splendor. As a result of this new infusion of light, the original idea is resurrected in all of its majesty and power. All who embrace it are elevated with its ascent. Even those who attached themselves to the idea in its fallen state are raised up, and they are inspired to a powerful, lofty t'shuva.

"This process will surely come about. The light of G-d, which is buried away in the fundamental point of Zion, and which is now concealed by clouds, will surely appear. From the lowly valley, it will raise up G-d's Temple and Kingdom and all of its branches. All those who cling to it, the near and the distant, will be uplifted with it, for a true revival and an everlasting salvation."[38]

At the turn of this century, as the Zionist movement grew in influence and attracted more and more followers, many religious Jews rose up in protest. In their eyes, the movement to resettle the Land of Israel was brazenly secular, even defiant of Torah. While Rabbi Kook exhorted the pioneers to return to a sanctified life of Torah,[39] he saw the inner source and positive side of their courageous endeavor. The return of the nation to Israel was in itself a great, holy act. Simply because they were Jews, in the depths of their proud Jewish souls, the Zionists also shared

---

with the goal of realizing his nation's most exalted yearning for spiritual greatness in all of its purity." *Orot HaT'shuva*, 4:5.

38. *Orot HaT'shuva*, 12:12.
39. *Orot, Orot Yisrael*, 4:3; Letters of Rabbi Kook, Vol. 1, pg. 183.

the yearning for a full Jewish life.[40] Their scorn of the commandments was a blemish that was destined to heal.

SPIRITUAL REBELLION

Rabbi Kook's deep spiritual insight did not blind him to the unholy lifestyles of the secular pioneers. However, he knew that the holy essence of *Am Yisrael* guaranteed that the nation would return to its roots. Long before the establishment of the State of Israel, Rabbi Kook described this process in almost prophetic terms:

"We recognize that a spiritual rebellion will come to pass in *Eretz Yisrael* amongst the people of Israel in the beginnings of the nation's revival. The material comfort which will be attained by a percentage of the nation, convincing them that they have already completely reached their goal, will constrict the soul, and days will come which will seem to be devoid of all spirit and meaning. The aspirations for lofty and holy ideals will cease, and the spirit of the nation will plunge and sink low until a storm of rebellion will appear, and people will come to see clearly that the power of Israel lies in its eternal holiness, in the light of G-d and His Torah, in the yearning for spiritual light which is the ultimate valor, triumphing over all of the worlds and all of their powers."[41]

In another essay, Rabbi Kook writes:

"Our nation will be built and reestablished; all of its foun-

---

40. *Orot, Eretz Yisrael,* 8. See *Lights on Orot,* Chapter 8.
41. *Orot,* pg. 84, para. 44.

dations will return to their full might, through the reactivating, strengthening, perfection, and spreading of its faith, its Divine inner holiness, and its reverence of G-d. All of the nation's builders will come to recognize this truth. Then with a mighty, valorous voice, they will call out to themselves and to their brethren, 'Let us come and return to the L-rd.' And this will be a true return. It will be a t'shuva filled with valor, a t'shuva which will give strength and vigor to all of the nation's spiritual and physical aspects, to all of the endeavors needed for the building and perfection of the people, inspiring it to rebirth and to stability. The nation's eyes will be opened, its soul will be cleansed, its light will shine, its wings will spread, a reborn nation will arise, a great, awesome, and numerous people, filled with the light of G-d and the majesty of nationhood. *Behold, the people shall rise up like a great lion, and like a young lion, it shall lift itself up.*"[42]

LAST STOP — JERUSALEM

It can be seen that the return of the Jewish people to the Land of Israel is a necessary stage in the t'shuva of the nation. It follows that a Jew who becomes a *baal t'shuva* in Chicago has only returned a part of the way home. While his personal character and behavior have been purified by the light of the Torah, he has traveled only half of the journey.[43] The "t'shuva train"

---

42. Numbers, 23:24; *Orot HaT'shuva*, 15:11.

43. See the *Kuzari*, 5:23, "*Eretz Yisrael* is especially distinguished by the L-rd of Israel, and deeds can only be perfect there. Many of the commandments given to the Jewish people do not apply to someone who does not live in the Land; and the heart will not be pure, and one's intention will not be completely devoted to G-d, except in the place

is continuing on to Israel. The final stop is Jerusalem. Every Jew needs to bring his little light home to the Holy Land where it can join the great flame. He has to raise up his private, individual life, to the higher life of the *Clal*, to merge his personal goals with the goals of the nation.[44] To rectify the blemish caused by *galut*, he has to stop being in exile and join the ingathered. He has to actualize the words of his prayers, "And gather us together from the four corners of the earth."[45]

Rabbi Kook writes that the true t'shuva of the Jewish people is in our return to *Eretz Yisrael*.[46] Again and again, in his letters and speeches, he called the Jewish people to return home to Zion. One public proclamation, sent out all over the Diaspora, years before the Holocaust, was entitled, "The Great Call."

THE GREAT CALL

"To the Land of Israel, Gentlemen, To the Land of Israel! Let us utter this appeal in one voice, in a great and never-ending cry.

"Come to the Land of Israel, dear brothers, come to the

which is known to be specially selected by G-d." Also there, 5:58, "The commandments must be performed in wholeness in order to be worthy of reward." See also, *Torat Eretz Yisrael*, Chapter One, pgs. 6-9, regarding *Emunah* and *Half-Emunah*.

44. "The first, fundamental step in t'shuva is to attach oneself with the soul of the nation...." *Orot HaT'shuva*, 4:7.

45. *Shemona Esrei* Prayer.

46. See the Essay, *T'shuva and Shalom*, Rabbi Kook, Appendix to *Orot HaT'shuva*, Ohr Etzion Edition, translated in the Appendix of this book.

Land of Israel. Save your souls, the soul of your generation, the soul of the entire nation; save her from desolation and destruction, save her from decay and degradation, save her from defilement and all evil — from all of the suffering and oppression that threatens to come upon her in all the lands of the world without exception or distinction....

"Escape with your lives and come to Israel; G-d's voice beckons us; His hand is outstretched to us; His spirit within our hearts unites us, encourages us and obliges us all to cry in a great, powerful and awesome voice: Brothers! Children of Israel, beloved and dear brethren, come to the Land of Israel, do not tarry with arrangements and official matters; rescue yourselves, gather, come to the Land of Israel...

"From the time we were exiled from our Land, the Torah has accompanied Israel into exile, wandering from Babylon to France, Spain, Germany, Eastern and Central Europe, Poland, Russia, and elsewhere. And now, how happy we would be if we were able to say that she has returned to her first place, to the Land of Israel, together with the people of Israel, which continues to multiply in the Holy Land.

"And now, who is so blind that he does not see the L-rd's hand guiding us in this, and does not feel obligated to work along with G-d? *A heavenly voice in the future will cry aloud on top of the mountains and say, 'Whoever has wrought with G-d, let him come and receive his reward.'*[47] Who can exempt himself from doing his part in bringing additional blessing and swifter salvation; from awakening many hearts to return to the Holy Land, to the

47. *Vayikra Rabbah*, 27:2

L-rd's legacy, that they may become a part of it, to settle it with enterprises and buildings, to purchase property, to plant and sow, to do everything necessary for the foundation of life of a stable and organized settlement...."[48]

BANNER OF JERUSALEM

Another public proclamation was addressed to Orthodox communities to urge their Aliyah to Israel. In establishing a movement called "The Banner of Jerusalem," Rabbi Kook called upon all religious Jews to come to Israel to rebuild the nation's spiritual life, just as the secular Zionists were rebuilding the physical.

"Jews! We call you to the sacred task of building our Jewish nation in our Holy Land, in *Eretz Yisrael*. Come to us, rally together under the "Banner of Jerusalem" which we now raise aloft before the whole Jewish religious public.

"We all know the 'Banner of Zion' which unites a certain portion of our brethren on the basis of our Jewish secular interests in the Land of Israel. But there are many who have not joined the union of those who bear the Zionist flag, and a great many who feel it impossible to do so. We simply record the plain fact that this is so, without questioning its veracity.

"Yet it cannot be that the largest, most natural, and earnest portion of Jewry, the majority of the Jewish religious public, should remain indifferent to the wonderful events of the pre-

48. For the full text of Rabbi Kook's letter, see the book, *Selected Letters*, translated and annotated by Tzvi Feldman, Ma'alot Publications.

sent, and not lend a hand in the holy task of building our nation on our sacred soil because of so-called objections....

"Jews, all the loyal believers in the Jewish faith, there can be no doubt that the Divine power is now manifesting itself in us amidst the great world events. We are certainly called to return to our ancient home in the Land of Israel, there to renew our ancient holy life....

"We religious Jews must all profoundly know and believe that the Divine hand is now leading us openly to our high, ideal destiny. We must make known to the whole world, the true meaning of the present wonderous happenings, whose purpose is so clearly the hastening of our redemption and salvation, from which alone will also spring forth the redemption and salvation of all mankind.

"With the flaming, illuminating, Divine faith, with all the luster of our holy Torah, with the vitality of all of the most refined and devout Jews, we shall carry our flag, the 'Banner of Jerusalem' by which alone the 'Banner of Zion' will also be properly hoisted. For the value of Jewish secular power will be elucidated to the world only in the light of our holy Jewish spiritual power, emphasized by the uplifted voices of the whole religious Jewish world community, setting with holy enthusiasm to the task of our national construction, of our return to the Land of Israel, by the grace of the Divine and illuminating light, *O House of Jacob, come, and let us walk in the light of the L-rd.*"[49]

49. See *Ma'amrei HaRiyah,* "The Banner of Jerusalem," Mosad HaRav Kook Publishers. For a translation of the full text, see Feldman's *Selected Letters,* cited above.

Chapter Eighteen

TORAH, TORAH, TORAH

BACK TO THE GOOD OLD DAYS

Phase two in the t'shuva of Israel is the nation's return to the Torah. During the reign of King Solomon, the nation of Israel was at its prime.[1] We lived in peace in our own homeland. A Jewish government ruled over the country from the majestic city of Jerusalem. All of the people gathered for the Festivals at the Temple three times a year. Jewish law went forth from the Sanhedrin. Prophets communicated the word of the L-rd to the nation. A powerful Jewish army guarded the country's borders. Torah was studied in great academies of learning. Hebrew was spoken on the street. The leaders of foreign nations flocked to Jerusalem to pay tribute to the Jews.[2]

When Israel was exiled, however, everything was lost. The

1. *Bamidbar Rabbah*, 13:14.
2. Kings I, 10:1.

country was conquered by enemies. Jerusalem was razed, the Temple destroyed. Prophecy ceased.[3] Jews wandered from country to country. They began speaking strange languages. Instead of being honored by the gentiles, the Jews were disgraced. They became an oppressed minority in other peoples' lands. And while Jews continued to learn Torah throughout their exile, its light was considerably waned.[4] In the face of persecution and assimilation, Judaism lost its once great stature.

As we mentioned in the previous chapter, with the commencement of the Zionist movement, the Jewish people began to return to what had been lost. Jews began to return to their homeland. They began to return to their very own Hebrew language. A Jewish government returned to Jerusalem. The city was rebuilt. Once again, Jews were sovereign in their homeland. Jewish soldiers once again guarded its borders. Once again, foreign rulers came to pay tribute to the leaders of Israel. The nation was resurrected to life. The physical, national body of Israel's statehood was restored with a newfound Jewish valor and strength. But without the Temple, without the Sanhedrin and prophecy, without the pilgrimages to Jerusalem three times a year, and without a national dedication to Torah, the return is still incomplete. Nonetheless, Rabbi Kook assures us, within the yearning to return to the Land is a deeper, hidden yearning to return to the Torah as well.

"Within the inner heart, in its pure and holy chambers, the Israeli flame increases, demanding the strong, brave, constant connection of life to all of the *mitzvot* of G-d.... And in the hearts

3.   Lamentations, 2:9.
4.   *Chagiga* 5B.

of all the empty (Jews), and in the hearts of all of the sinners of Israel, the fire burns and blazes in the most inward depths, and in the nation in its entirety, all of the desire for freedom, and all of the yearning for life, for the community and for the individual, all of the hope for redemption, only from the source of this inner spring of life do they flow in order to live Israeli life in its fullest, without contradiction or limitation."[5]

HIDDEN TREASURE

Under the secular-looking Zionist State is a flaming, raging, engulfing fireball of t'shuva. The Jewish soul is yearning for religion. Like a man dying of thirst in the desert, the voice of the nation cries out, "Torah, Torah, Torah." Ironically, it is precisely the spiritual wilderness which brings the great thirst.

"T'shuva will come (to the Jewish nation) in several directions. One of the causes will be the deep sorrow felt over the humiliation inflicted upon the great spiritual treasure which our forefathers bequeathed to us, and which possesses immeasurable power and glory."[6]

Israel's great spiritual treasure is the Torah, the commandments, the holidays, Jewish customs, traditions, prayer, and the vast sea of Talmudic learning.

"This mighty spirit spans over all generations. Its source is

5.   *Orot*, *Eretz Yisrael*, 8. See, *Lights on Orot*, Chapter Eight.
6.   *Orot HaT'shuva*, 4:9.

the most exalted Divine Source of life. When one looks to it, one finds everything, all beauty and splendor."[7]

A story is told about a poor man from a poor village who was told in a dream to seek out a treasure buried under a certain bridge in a faraway town. The poor man made the long journey and located the bridge. As he was searching around, a policeman accosted him and demanded to know what he was doing. When the poor man explained, the policeman confided that he too had had a similar foolish dream, in which a treasure was to be found in a ceratin faraway village under the shack of a poor man. When the policeman cited the poor man's name and village, the poor man realized that the treasure was buried under his very own house! He had to journey to the bridge to discover the secret. Sure enough, when the poor man hurried back home, he uncovered the treasure under the floor of his storeroom.[8]

In much the same manner, the Jewish people have lost sight of the treasure of their ancestral past. Seduced by the gentile cultures around us, we have very often ignored our own pure, holy spring, for pools of polluted water.

This cultural assimilation has occurred throughout our dispersion. Even in the Holy Land, the symbols, influences, and values of Western society abound. The immigrants returning to Israel brought back, not only their pure Jewish souls, but also a lot of foreign baggage. Socialism, communism, atheism, capitalism, bohemianism, materialism, and secularism are only some of the travel stickers we have collected along our journey. One day,

7.   Ibid.

8.   *Siach Sarfei Kodesh*, recounted by Rabbi Nachman of Breslov.

Rabbi Kook assures us, a feeling of shame will cause us to return to our original love, the Torah.

"The darkness of heresy caused our people to detach themselves from this rich meadow and to stumble in foreign pastures which have absolutely no life nor vitalizing substance for us. The pain of this great anguish will burst awesomely forth, clearing the way for sensibility and reason to know what positive elements might be retrieved from all the false paths which led us astray. The soul's inner longing for holiness will be freed. It will break out of its prison, and with a powerful thirst, every awakened spirit will begin to drink deeply from the original, exalted life source."[9].

TORAH TAPES

With a return to the Torah, the Jewish people erase all of the foreign concepts and values which have tainted Jewish identity and culture during our long exile in gentile lands, and replace them with a library of holy Torah tapes and texts. Rather than being divided between two separate worlds, a Jew at home and a German or Frenchman on the street, we return to our unique Jewish wholeness. We come to hear clearly the voice of our souls calling us back to our G-d. Embracing our holiness, we long for a life of Torah, a life of moral purity, a life cleansed from sin. With each Torah verse that we learn, with each Mishna, with each page of *Gemara*, we give revitalizing Jewish nourishment to our long-neglected souls.

9.   *Orot HaT'shuva*, 4:9.

BACK TO THE BOOK OF BOOKS

To accomplish such a vast, national t'shuva, Rabbi Kook writes that a broad system of popular Torah education is needed. After having abandoned our unique Jewish treasure for so many years, we have a lot of relearning to do. In fact, many Jews returning to Judaism have to start at the very beginning by learning the *alef bet*.

"From a moral point-of-view, the innate fear of transgression is the healthiest human disposition. This quality stands out in the Jewish people, in its natural aversion to any sin or wrongdoing in opposition to the Torah and the commandments, which are the inheritance of the community of Jacob. This disposition will only return to the Jewish people through national program of Torah learning, both in producing outstanding Torah scholars, and in establishing fixed times of daily learning for the masses. It is impossible for the Jewish people to return to their natural life, in all of its breadth and stature, if it will not also return to its spiritual nature, in all of its fullness, including the all-important fear of sin which, when healthy, brings remorse and t'shuva in its wake. With the strengthening of the nation's vitality in all of its facets, its restless confusion will cease, and its national institutions will all return to their natural moral focus, so unique and deep-seated in Israel, to differentiate with a hair-splitting exactness between the forbidden and the permitted. Then all the detailed laws of the Torah and the Sages will be recognized as the necessary foundation for an independent Jewish life, without which a vital national existence is impossible."[10]

10. *Orot HaT'shuva*, 6:3.

As we shall learn in Chapter Nineteen, the holiness of the Jewish nation is expressed in our yearning for absolute morality, goodness, and universal justice. To accomplish this on a national level, in day-to-day life, high-sounding platitudes are not enough. To be a holy nation, holiness must be grounded in every aspect of life. Morality must shine in all spheres of endeavor. Only in this manner can all of life be sanctified and uplifted. How can this be achieved? Only by Israel's commitment to all of the Divine laws of Sinai. It is the detailed commandments, in all of their exact measure and precision, which embody G-d's will for the world. Only the Divine law of the Torah can provide the foundation for a pure Jewish life, by establishing guidelines for every aspect of our lives, from the food we eat, to the type of clothes we wear, to our dealings in business, our personal behavior, and our national priorities and goals.

SECRETS OF TORAH

However, a simple learning of Torah is not enough to return us completely to our roots. After a two-thousand year exile, we have to undergo a profound, inner transformation in order to truly become *a kingdom of priests and a holy nation.*[11] A change in external behavior is not enough. When we return to our roots, the transformation must affect our personalities, our thought processes, and our innermost aspirations.

"To strengthen these foundations, we need to endear the hearts of our people to the light of the true, inner Torah, the secrets of Torah, which, because of their influence on students who had not been properly prepared, brought about their rejection

11. Exodus, 19:6.

and scorn. It is, however, from this life-giving light... that the world's lasting salvation will sprout. The appearance of this exalted, benevolent light will revitalize both the nation and the individual, to *raise the fallen tabernacle of David,*[12] and to *remove the shame of the people of G-d from all of the earth.*"[13]

Rabbi Kook is careful to warn that only a Torah student with the proper background of learning can safely delve into the deep waters of Kabbalah. Nonetheless, it is precisely the mystical side of Torah which gives Israel the high-octane fuel it needs to sustain the long and difficult task of national rebuilding.[14] Rabbi Kook himself was a master of Kabbalah. The profound insights found throughout all of his writings, his towering love for all of mankind, and his understanding of the unity of all creation, stem in great measure from this source. His teachings reveal how the inner formulations of Torah are at work in our time, bringing the national t'shuva of Israel ever-and-ever closer. By illuminating the inner blueprint of existence which is secretly active, guiding all things toward completion, Rabbi Kook helps us to set our lives on the ultimate course of perfection and joy.

"True complete t'shuva necessitates exalted horizons of meditation, an ascent to the supernal realm which is filled with truth and holiness. One can attain this only through the study of the inner dimensions of Torah and Divine wisdom dealing with the mystical understanding of the world. This demands physical and moral purity, so that the darkness of lusts will not pollute the lucidness of the intellect. But the study of Torah must precede all

---

12. Amos 9:11.
13. Isaiah, 25:8; *Orot HaT'shuva,* 4:9.
14. Introduction of Rav Chaim Vital to *Etz Chaim.*

other disciplines, especially the study of the transcendental Torah, for only it can break down all of the iron-like, material barriers separating the individual and the community from their Father in heaven."[15]

Ours is a very material generation. Living in a capitalistic, consumer-oriented society, we are bombarded by material messages. Like one of Pavlov's dogs, we are trained to want more money, nicer clothes, a bigger house, a newer car. This obsession with the material world can block out spiritual light completely. **Only an intense inner purification, and a connection to transcendental realms, can free us from the physical lusts which block our connection to G-d.** Thus t'shuva and the secrets of Torah go hand-in-hand, each one lighting the path for the other.[16]

In another essay, Rabbi Kook explains why the mystical understandings of Torah are vital to Israel's rise toward national rebirth.[17] The Talmud states that preceding the *Mashiach* there will be great *chutzpah* in the world.[18] This *chutzpah* is an insolence directed against Judaism. It is a brazenness which seeks to negate everything holy and Divine. Before the truth of the Torah is finally revealed, there will be a great darkness. Torah scholars will be held in contempt. The teachings of Judaism will be scorned. This comes about because, as the time of *Mashiach* draws near, the world is ready to embrace a universal vision of unity, where all particulars are recognized as part of the whole. In contrast, the Torah is seen as a code of primitive details, something specifically

15. *Orot HaT'shuva*, 10:1.
16. See *Orot HaT'shuva*, 10:8 and 10:9.
17. *Orot HaT'shuva*, 4:10.
18. *Sotah* 49B.

Jewish, bounded on all sides with restrictions, with no connection to the wide world and its seemingly infinite horizons.

For example, a universal yearning for unity can be seen in the great popularity of Internet. From his home computer, a person can now be connected to all of the world. He is no longer just a name in a phonebook, but an active player in a complex, international game. Thanks to advances in communications, he has the knowledge of the world at his fingertips. On his private, home screen, he can see from one end of the globe to the other. And people all over the world can also find out about him.

While the world is striving toward cosmic oneness, the Torah, to the uninitiated, seems to be preoccupied with unimportant details, with keeping kosher and not letting women wear pants. This viewpoint occurs when the Torah is looked at in a myopic fashion, precept by precept, law after law, with the focus on an individual's behavior. However, to an experienced "surfer" in the great sea of Torah, what expanses of unity and wholeness lie under each individual command! What endless horizons and waves! What mind-expanding revelations of oneness, not only of this world, but of all the spiritual worlds which constitute and surround all of existence! In the Torah, one can find all of life's secrets.

"If people studied the Torah in this light, to broaden their spiritual ken, in order to understand the connection between the details of life and the universal, spiritual realms of existence, then t'shuva would come, and the perfection of the world would follow in its wake.... We must employ a higher healing, to add strength to our spiritual talents, to understand in a clear, straightforward, down-to-earth manner, the connection between the teachings and commandments of the Torah, and the highest, most universal ideas. Then the power of the spiritual life will be renewed in the world, in practice and theory, and a movement of general t'shuva will begin to blossom and bloom."[19]

TORAH OF REDEMPTION

We have mentioned that t'shuva and redemption run along two parallel, overlapping paths. Since Torah is so integral to t'shuva, it is not surprising to discover that it is precisely the secrets of Torah which pave the way for the redemption of Israel.[20] The opposite is also true. **Rabbi Kook writes that it is precisely the dry, superficial learning of Torah which causes the nation to become habituated, and even comfortable, with life in for eign lands.**

"By being alienated from the recognition of the secrets of Torah, the *Kedusha* of *Eretz Yisrael* is understood in a confused, unfocused fashion. By alienating oneself from the secrets of G-d, the highest treasures of the deep Divine life become extraneous, secondary matters which do not enter the depths of the soul, and as a result, the most potent force of the individual's and the nation's soul will be missing, and the exile is found to be pleasant in its own accord. For to someone who only comprehends the superficial level, nothing basic will be lacking in the absence of the Land of Israel, the Jewish Kingdom, and all of the facets of the nation in its built form.

19 *Orot HaT'shuva*, 4:10.
20. See the *Even Shlema*, 11:3, by the Gaon of Vilna, "The redemption will not come except through the learning of Torah, and the core of the redemption depends on the learning of Kabbalah."

"For him, the foundation of yearning for salvation is like a side branch that cannot be united with the deep understanding of Judaism, and this itself testifies to the poverty of insight which is found in this juiceless perspective.

"We are not rejecting any form of study or contemplation which is founded on truthfulness, on sensitivity of thought, or on the fear of Heaven, in whatever form it takes; but only rejecting the specific aspect of this perspective which seeks to negate the secrets of Torah and their great influence on the spirit of the nation — for this is a tragedy which we are obligated to fight against with counsel and wisdom, with holiness and valor."[21]

Basically, Rabbi Kook is saying that it is not enough for a Jew to study only about the commandments which effect his personal everyday life. He must also learn about the more encompassing concepts of Judaism like the role of the nation of Israel in perfecting the world, the meaning of *Eretz Yisrael* to the nation, the centrality of Jerusalem to Judaism, the importance of prophecy, the Temple, and the deeper understandings of the ingathering of the exiles. If he does not immerse himself in these studies, then he will not miss their absence, and he will be content with his life of exile in foreign lands.[22]

Elsewhere in the book *Orot*, Rabbi Kook writes:

"The secrets of Torah bring the redemption and return Israel to its Land, because the Torah of truth in its mighty inner logic

21. *Orot, Eretz Yisrael*, 2.
22. For a detailed discussion of this theme, see the book *Lights on Orot*, Chapter Two.

demands the complete soul of the nation. Through this inner To-rah, the nation begins to feel the pain of exile and to realize the absolute impossibility for its character to fulfill its potential as long as it is oppressed on foreign soil. As long as the light of the supernal Torah is sealed and bound, the inner need to return to Zion will not stir itself with deep faith."[23]

Thus we learn that a national return to Torah and to the Land of Israel are necessary for the complete t'shuva of both the individual Jew and the nation. Living a religious life in the Di-aspora is not to be taken as the end of the journey. It is the com-bination of a life of Torah in *Eretz Yisrael* which brings the Jewish people to perfection, and which returns the light of G-d to the world.[24] As Rabbi Kook writes, "The Judaism of *Eretz Yisruel* is the salvation itself."[25]

23. *Orot*, pg. 95, para. 64. For a full translation, see *Celebrations of the Soul*, pg. 207, translation by Pesach Yaffe, Genesis Jerusalem Press. See also, *Tikuney Zohar*, 30.

24. *Kuzari*, 5:23.

25. *Orot, Eretz Yisrael*, 1.

Chapter Nineteen

LIGHT UNTO THE NATIONS

We have seen how the t'shuva of the Jewish people includes a return to national sovereignty in *Eretz Yisrael* and a return to Torah. The holy nation, living a holy life of Torah, in the Holy Land, is the combination that spreads the light of G-d to all of the world. What will this new, *baal t'shuva* nation be like? What will be its character, its principles, its culture? What will be its aspirations and goals? When we know who we are destined to be, we can guide our lives to be in line with our nation's highest ideals.

TRUTH, JUSTICE, AND THE ISRAELITE WAY

Remember Superman? The champion of "truth, justice, and the American way." Today, at least for a grown-up, it is obvious that the American way is not one of justice, nor truth. However, as long as American culture dominates modern civilization, the world has to live with this myth. **In the future, the real Superman**

will be found — the nation of Israel — championing truth, justice, and the Israelite way.[1] What is the Israelite way? Torah. In the past, with the giving of the Torah at Sinai, the nation of Israel brought the concepts of morality and Divine justice to a barbaric world. So too in the future, the People of the Book will once again educate the rest of mankind. This is our national calling.

"The apex of the nation's soul is the yearning for universal good. The striving for it is built into the essence of its being, and this influences all of existence. The highest concept of t'shuva is imbedded in this exalted hidden source."[2]

Rabbi Kook tells us that the essence of Israel's soul is the yearning for universal morality. This can be seen throughout Jewish history. Not only were we the first nation to uproot idol worship from the world, the Jewish people gave mankind a detailed code of law by which to live, based on the principle of justice. Jewish law and ethics cover all aspects of human endeavor, from property rights, civil law, damages, claims, marriage, employment, inheritance, trusteeship, laws of witnesses, and the like. These laws, and the moral codes which stem from them, became the foundations of Western civilization. The striving for justice is rooted in the Israeli soul. The Torah gives it its outward expression. It takes Israel's potential and actualizes it in life. **But even when the Jewish people are not keeping the Torah, G-d forbid,**

1. For an in-depth discussion on the fall of modern Western culture and the rise of the holy culture of Israel, see *War and Peace*, Chapter Eight, Rabbi David Samson and Tzvi Fishman.
2. *Orot HaT'shuva*, 4:6. Also, *Orot*, pg. 139, para. 5, "Knesset Yisrael yearns to live precisely in order to further the moral perfection of all existence...."

just their presence in the world reminds mankind of the standards of morality and justice which the nation of Israel gave birth to.

CONNECTION TO THE NATION

"The (basis of the) soul of the Jewish nation is absolute justice, which, to be achieved, demands the moral perfection of everything in the world. Thus, every moral blemish on the part of an individual Jew weakens his connection to the nation. The primary, fundamental t'shuva is to attach oneself to the soul of the people. With this, it is necessary to correct all of one's deeds, according to the essence of the nation's soul."[3]

A Jew is much more than an individual. He is attached with a living link to the Jewish nation as a whole. Beyond his own private existence, he is bound up with the life of the nation, or *clal*. **Thus, the primary t'shuva for a Jew is to bind himself to the soul of the people, which means putting his own personal life in line with the high moral strivings of the nation.**

"An individual cannot be connected to the root of the Jewish nation unless his soul has been purified through t'shuva of its coarse, human behavior and degenerate moral traits, or unless his soul is pure from the outset. For the fundamental character of the Jewish nation is the desire that the highest standard of justice, the justice of G-d, will be established in the world.

"Whoever has been blemished by any kind of transgression, to the extent of the blemish, the will for justice and goodness will

3.   *Orot HaT'shuva*, 4:7.

199

not function within him in a wholehearted fashion. Thus, he will not be truly attached with the national character of the Jewish people until the blemish has been erased."[4]

"To remove the barriers which prevent the perfection of a Jewish person's character, it is necessary to do away with every concrete obstruction which darkens the Jewish soul. This goal demands complete t'shuva for all of the specific acts of misconduct and sin, on the basis of the Written and Oral Law, all of which embody the Divine soul of the Jew."[5]

Rabbi Kook teaches that in order to reach the high level of personal perfection where an individual truly yearns for universal justice, he must bind himself with the soul of the Jewish nation. This can only be achieved if he cleanses himself from all transgression, not in a vague, general manner, but in a comprehensive spiritual overhaul based on all the fine tunings of Jewish law.

"A Jew must be united with the Divine good in the soul of the nation of Israel, and this will assist him in doing t'shuva. Always, he will be faced with his failings and sins, which arise from his alienation from the nation of G-d, which is the root of his being, and the source of all the good within him."[6]

When a Jew attaches himself to the soul of the nation, he plugs himself into a powerhouse of goodness. By identifying with the Jewish people, by getting involved in Jewish causes, by going to synagogue, by being interested in what's happening in Israel,

4. *Orot HaT'shuva*, 13:1
5. Ibid, 13:2.
6. Ibid, 13:3.

or by simply learning Hebrew, he becomes a better person. No matter what his station in life, he can feel good that he is a Jew. "I am a Jew, and I'm proud," should be his feeling every morning. Thus, there are two paths to becoming a champion of justice and truth. One can first correct all of his wrongdoings and personal blemishes and then attach oneself to the ideals of the nation; or he can attach himself to the ideals of the nation and subsequently bring his behavior into line with the Torah's precise code of laws. Should it arise in the mind that in cleaving to the soul of the nation, one will also be attaching oneself with the sinners of Israel, Rabbi Kook explains that this is not so.

"He should not hesitate to attach himself with the soul of the nation, even though there are evil and base individuals within it. This does not lessen in any manner the Divine light of good in the nation as a whole — for even in the lowest sinners of Israel, there is a spark of the Divine. Since the nation of Israel embodies the Divine good, not only for itself, but for the whole world, and all of existence, by connecting himself firmly with the soul of the nation, he will come to attach himself to the living G-d, and be in harmony with the Divine blessing which fills all of life. The light of G-d will then surround him in all of its splendor and power."[7]

T'SHUVA IS THE MESSAGE

Just as American materialism dominates world culture today, in the future, Israel's yearning for morality and universal justice will spread to the ends of the globe. Emulating the Jews, people will strive to be good. Everyone will want to serve G-d. Enlight-

7.   Ibid.

ened by the message of t'shuva, everyone will want to be like the Jews.

In those days, it shall come to pass, that ten men out of all of the languages of the nations shall take hold and seize the garment of a Jew, saying, We will go with you, for we have heard that G-d is with you.[8]

8.   Zachariah, 8:23.

Chapter Twenty

LIGHTS OF T'SHUVA

Rabbi Kook's notebooks are filled with essays, meditations, and insights that came to him as flashes of illumination in the course of his busy days. Since Rabbi Kook's reflections span all facets of t'shuva, we are listing a selection of them here, as beacons to help the *baal t'shuva* on his way. Some will seem immediately illuminating, while others will be meaningful to the reader only after he deepens his t'shuva experience.[1]

MEDIOCRITY WON'T SUFFICE

Just as a person must refine his evil attributes and thoughts

---

1. For the sake of clarity, instead of presenting difficult, word-for-word translations, many of the teachings have been paraphrased and condensed. All of the following sources, unless otherwise noted, are from *Orot HaT'shuva*.

toward their original purity, he must also raise mediocre attributes and thoughts toward the light of greatness.[2]

ELEVATING THE LOWLY TOWARD THE HEIGHTS

The work of elevating what is lowly in life toward perfection never ceases.[3]

HONOR OF G-D

The highest form of t'shuva is t'shuva for the sake of honoring G-d.[4]

REVENGE OF THE BODY

Sometimes, when a person attempts to cling to the heights of spirituality and the world of lofty thoughts, there is a danger that he will become disoriented from his physical nature, and his body will be influenced by evil factors. Rabbi Kook teaches that in order to engage in the higher realms of spiritualism, a person must first concentrate on his physical health and moral purity, cleansing himself of pride, anger, envy and the like. Once a person does t'shuva on a personal level, then he can direct his energies more toward the lofty yearnings for spiritual ascent.[5]

2.　14:1.
3.　Ibid.
4.　4:8.
5.　14:2.

NOTHING CAN STAND IN THE WAY

Nothing can stand in the way of t'shuva. The will of t'shuva is so great, it can overcome all barriers.[6]

THE SMALLEST TO THE GREATEST

A person should not look askance at any small matter which needs mending, no matter how insignificant it may seem in his eyes. Nor should a person refrain from striving for the heights, saying that exalted levels are beyond his grasp. Both the trivial and the cosmic are all a part of the same edifice.[7]

WORLD UNITY

Everything is united in the all-encompassing world of t'shuva.[8]

DON'T BE DISCOURAGED

The difficulties which one encounters in redressing one's shortcomings and sins should not be allowed to discourage a person from his pathway of t'shuva.[9]

OVERCOMING OBSTACLES

When a person is determined to do t'shuva, he may be faced

6. 14:3.
7. Ibid.
8. Ibid.
9. 14:4.

with barriers that impede his progress to the point where he feels he cannot mend all his wrongs. If, nonetheless, he holds firmly to his will for t'shuva, he will eventually overcome all of the things which stand in his way. Then the light of this "pent-up"[10] t'shuva will appear in all of its greatness, and in breaking out of its confinement and shackles, it will shine with a mighty force, becoming an exalted form of t'shuva....[11]

THE STRIVING FOR T'SHUVA

The striving for t'shuva alone is in itself t'shuva, and it has the power to create a person anew.[12]

THOUGHTS

Thoughts themselves have the power to mend.[13]

THE MOST IMPORTANT THING IN THE WORLD

Even if there are things which seem impossible to correct, let the person take comfort in the knowledge that by embracing t'shuva, he has achieved the most important thing in the world.[14]

---

10. A more literal translation might be "retroactive t'shuva."
11. 15:8.
12. Ibid.
13. Ibid.
14. Ibid.

SPIRITUAL REALITY

T'shuva leads a person to discover the true spiritual essence of the world.[15]

DEATH

The deeper a person's level of t'shuva, his fear of death lessens and totally recedes.[16]

T'SHUVA IS EASY

The major spiritual falls result from not believing how simple it is to do t'shuva.[17]

LOVE THOSE SINS

There is an exalted level of t'shuva when the recollection of one's sins does not cause chagrin, but rather unbelievable joy. This occurs when the person realizes that his sins served as catalysts to t'shuva, to raise him to a higher level and to a greater attachment to G-d.[18]

NO ROOM FOR EVIL

A person who does t'shuva motivated by a powerful love

15. 11:3.
16. Ibid.
17. 14:4a.
18. 8:2.

for G-d will come to see clearly that all of the world is a spiritual unity, filled with G-d's goodness alone.[19]

OVEREATING

If a person should eat in a gluttonous manner, or without the proper motivation, and immediately repent, his eating is elevated toward holiness like the bread-offerings eaten by the *Kohanim*.[20]

JOY

Thoughts of holiness and t'shuva that bring on sadness should be avoided. One is to serve G-d with joy.[21]

DOWN TO EARTH

People who are thoughtful and spiritual by nature often feel estranged from the world of action. As part of their t'shuva, these people should channel their spiritual talents into the practical world, to bring light to the physical realm as well.[22]

T'SHUVA BOOKS

If a person feels that certain forms of t'shuva suggested by

19.   12:5.
20.   14:8-10. Also 14:5.
21.   14:11.
22.   14:12.

books on moral improvement do not apply to his spiritual level, let him concentrate on things which seem closer to his grasp.[23]

TRAVEL EVERY HIGHWAY

A person should not completely ignore the different approaches to t'shuva which he finds written in books, for all pathways are good and ultimately connected. Together they form one whole.[24]

HIGHER AND HIGHER

The person involved in t'shuva must not remain static on any level, but must always strive to greater heights.[25] *A person must always ascend in the realm of holiness.*[26]

GOT TO KEEP MOVING

The natural contrition that burns in the heart from the experience of t'shuva evolves from the pain which the soul feels when it has remained static, when it should have constantly ascended higher and higher, in line with its true nature. However, this raging fire can be turned into a flame of great love filled

---

23. 14:15.
24. Ibid.
25. 14:16.
26. *Berachot* 28A. In his commentary on Proverbs, 15:25, the Gaon of Vilna writes: "A man is called a moving creature because one must always move from level to level; and if he will not rise to the next level, he will fall, G-d forbid, for it is impossible to remain forever static."

with exalted delight, when the soul will find the strength to return to its constant aim of ascending.[27]

TRUTH

The feeling of truth is the foundation of t'shuva.[28]

SELF-CRITICISM

Self-criticism, when it delves deeply into the essence of one's being, and examines thoroughly every action and thought, deepens the feeling of contrition over the absence of truth in one's life, and makes the person feel his disgrace, ugliness, and nothingness. Then the person does t'shuva out of a love for the light of truth.[29]

SLOW BUT SURE

If a person who achieved his high level through study and good deeds should suffer a spiritual decline, he must raise himself slowly in gradual stages, in the same manner which he originally ascended the spiritual ladder.[30]

SPIRITUAL PEOPLE

If a person who has attained spiritual heights due to the innate loftiness of his soul should fall, he must raise himself up

27. 15:3.
28. 15:1.
29. Ibid.
30. 14:17.

with a swift, mighty leap vaulting over stages. Yet, even in this exalted form of t'shuva, attention must be given to smaller, detailed matters, though these are not the main focus of t'shuva for a person endowed with an enlightened spiritual disposition.[31]

HOLY THOUGHTS

A baal t'shuva must walk in higher paths, in the paths of righteousness and holy thoughts.[32]

HOSTILITY

Every sin, even the smallest transgression, instills hatred in a person toward some creature, and through t'shuva, love returns to its place.[33]

THE HOLINESS OF LIFE

Every spiritual level and conception of life is filled with a treasure of holiness.[34]

STAGES

When a person leaps toward exalted visions, beyond his ap-

31. Ibid.
32. 14:37.
33. 12:4. Rabbi Filber explains that sin shatters the harmony between the individual and the world, causing division and estrangement which leads to animosity and hatred. Loc. cit., pg. 121, nt. 16.
34. 14:18.

propriate state, he fails to acquire the aspects of holiness in the lower stages, which are more in line with his level. At the same time, since the lofty visions are too spiritual for him, he cannot hold on to them permanently. Therefore, he must return in t'shuva to the levels which he skipped, without forgetting the higher light. Then everything will be raised up to goodness.[35]

THE EVIL INCLINATION

The more a person devotes himself to serving G-d and pursuing a righteous path, the more his evil inclination fights to tempt him with lusts. He must proceed with even greater devotion. He must not be afraid of anything.[36]

LOFTY VISIONS

If a lofty vision seems beyond our reach, we should know that the barrier is only physical, and not due to spiritual causes. We must not let discouragement dampen our will. The longing for the heights itself raises us and brings us closer to our ideals.[37]

IS DEPRESSION WEIGHING YOU DOWN?

Should a person lack faith in the value of prayer, not because he lacks faith in G-d, but because his spirit is weighed down by his depression over his sins, and by the pain involved in t'shuva, this will ultimately be transformed into a great, ex-

35. Ibid.
36. 14:19.
37. 14:21.

alted faith in G-d's compassion, which will grant him a wonderous salvation.[38]

PRAYER

Just as nothing can stand in the way of t'shuva, nothing can stand in the way of prayer.[39]

THE POWER OF PRAYER

Though there are barriers which impede prayer, the person who is faced with them, yet continues to call out to G-d, believing firmly in the power of prayer, for him all of the barriers will finally fall away. Then the light of prayer which was smothered by the barriers will burst mightily forth, with an exalted strength, forging paths for myriads of prayers which were blocked – both his prayers and the prayers of all people.[40]

CRYING OUT TO G-D

Prayer, crying out to G-d, and t'shuva from the depths of the heart, actualized in the correction of one's deeds, all of these must precede the attainment of every higher perception.[41]

38. 14:22.
39. 15:8.
40. Ibid.
41. 10:11.

A NEW BEING

The moment there is a striving for t'shuva, t'shuva occurs, and the person becomes a new being.[42]

TORAH STUDY

A lack of enjoyment in the study of Torah is a sign of a blemish in the soul. The moment a Jew thinks to improve this shortcoming, the soul's natural, exalted light of holiness returns and shines, and the joy of Torah is revealed.[43]

TORAH TIPS

To the degree that a person has thoughts of t'shuva before studying Torah, whether regarding his previous learning, his deeds, or his life in general, his learning will be clearer and filled with greater understanding.[44]

When a person does t'shuva out of a great love and clear recognition of G-d, his Torah learning is endowed by G-d with a depth and fruitfulness which cannot be found in any other learning.[45]

KABBALAH

It is only after a course of complete t'shuva that a person

42. 14:4.
43. 14:26.
44. 14:27.
45. 14:28.

can enter the spiritual world of Kabbalah and glimpse its supernal light.[46]

EVERYTHING IN THE WORLD

Everything in the world helps raise the spirit to the loftiest heights of t'shuva: all of the Torah, all of science, every manifestation of physical prowess, every knowledge of the world and of life, every contact with mankind, every honest and righteous trait.[47]

SHORTCOMINGS

When a person experiences inner shame over a shortcoming in any sphere whatsoever, he must carefully search to discover what is missing and work to repair it – not in a superficial manner, for this will only bring upon further decline, but with a spirit of courage and penetrating self-probing.[48]

THOU SHALL NOT DELAY

One must hasten to return in t'shuva for every sin, even the most insignificant, because a delay in t'shuva is like a delay in removing impurity from the Temple, or in removing a mixture of linen and wool from a garment, or in removing *chametz* from one's domain on Passover. For every second of delay is a sin

---

46.   10:8 and 10:9. And see, *Orot HaKodesh,* Part One, pg. 261.
47.   *Orot HaT'shuva,* 14:29.
48.   Ibid.

by itself, and the multiplication of small sins becomes a serious matter.[49]

GUARD YOUR TONGUE

A person who has achieved a high level of spirituality must do t'shuva for every unnecessary word which left his lips; even for every essential, holy utterance, if it lacked the proper intention.[50]

EREV SHABBAT

Before the Sabbath, a person should do t'shuva for everything that took place during the week, so that he can receive the holiness of the Sabbath without the obstructions which result from his sins.[51]

MOTZEI SHABBAT

At the conclusion of the Sabbath, one must do t'shuva on matters which were overshadowed by the holiness of the day, so that they not interfere with the activities of the week, when the holy light of the Sabbath cannot protect him.[52]

RETURN TO THE WORLD

It is precisely after a true, pure inspiration of t'shuva that

49. 14:32.
50. Ibid.
51. 14:33.
52. Ibid.

a person must return to the world and to an active involvement in life. This returns holiness to its proper place and causes the Divine Presence to reign in the world.[53]

WISDOM

It is forbidden to separate the fear of G-d from wisdom. Similarly, wisdom must shed its light on every detailed aspect of the fear of G-d. Man's soul will be illuminated from the proper union of these two lights, and t'shuva, joy, and life will come to the world.[54]

THE FOUNDATION OF WISDOM

T'shuva from all transgression is the foundation of Jewish wisdom.[55]

MISSION IMPOSSIBLE

When a person longs to be nothing less than completely righteous, it will be difficult for him to be a *baal t'shuva*.[56]

IMMERSED IN T'SHUVA

A man should always aspire to be a *baal t'shuva* whose thoughts are immersed in t'shuva, and who strives to actualize the ideals of t'shuva in his life. In this way, his t'shuva will el-

---

53. 14:30.
54. 14:34.
55. *Orot HaKodesh*, Part Three, *Musar HaKodesh*, pg. 20.
56. *Orot HaT'shuva*, 14:36.

evate him toward the heights, to the degree of the completely righteous, and even higher.[57]

THE RIGHTEOUS

People who were born with a natural proclivity to be righteous, if they should happen to sin, they can return to their previous paths of righteousness without any obvious increase in their efforts to maintain a constant holy striving.[58]

THE SUMMONS TO BE HOLY

People who by nature have souls constantly in need of t'shuva, they are the ones who are summoned to be saintly and holy men.[59]

THE VALUE OF THOUGHT

Sometimes the spirit falls into a lowly state, and a man cannot find pleasure in life because his sins weigh on his mind, and because of a lack of good deeds or Torah study. This person must strive to hold on to the secret power of thought and realize that G-d values thoughts more than all sacrifices and burnt offerings.[60]

57. Ibid.
58. 14:37.
59. Ibid.
60. 14:38. *Zohar, Parshat Naso,* 121.

THE SECRETS OF CONTEMPLATION

A person should strengthen himself with the realization that at times a lack of good deeds and Torah study results from a person's great penchant to the secrets of contemplation, and it may be that his depression is due in large measure to his not properly appreciating the significance of his meditations. He should strive to understand with a deeper knowledge that the perfection of the world, and the healing of all souls, all depend on the foundation of thought.[61]

ROCKET MAN

A person should elevate his thoughts as much as he can, and he will rise with them to a t'shuva filled with a great love of G-d.[62]

TZADDIKIM

There are *tzaddikim* who feel that their souls are filled with the pain of sin if, for even one moment, they should lack a full, exalted cleaving to G-d. These are the righteous for whom the secrets of G-d will always be revealed.[63]

JEWISH LITERATURE

The feelings of t'shuva in all of their magnificence, with all of their spiritual depth, must be revealed in literature, in order

61. *Orot HaT'shuva*, 14:38.
62. Ibid.
63. 14:39.

that the generation of Israel's revival will learn in the depths of its being the life-giving powers of t'shuva, leading it to a spiritual return and healing.[64]

POET OF T'SHUVA

There will certainly arise for us a poet of t'shuva, who will be a poet of life, a poet of Israel's rebirth, a poet of the nation's soul as it advances toward redemption.[65]

PRIDE

As long as one has pride in his heart, he cannot do proper t'shuva.[66]

G-D MADE ME DO IT

As long as a person has not returned in t'shuva, he carries the guilt for his transgressions. When he embarks on a path of t'shuva, all of his sins are removed, and G-d takes responsibility for them. In the light of the clear perception which t'shuva brings, the baal t'shuva comes to see that the sins of his past were Divinely inspired.[67]

---

64. 17:5.
65. Ibid. See also, 17:3, and 15:12. Certainly, more than anyone else in our time, Rabbi Kook himself has been the poet of the nation's rebirth – Ed.
66. *Musar Avicha, Midot HaRiyah*, Pride, para. 4, Mosad HaRav Kook Publishers.
67. 16:1a.

FEAR

If a person is so afraid of the magnitude of his sins that he cannot bring himself to confront his past and bring his life into order, this in itself is the root of consolement – the feeling of fear means that the process of t'shuva is underway, and that salvation is near.[68]

IF YOU FEEL BAD, FEEL GOOD

If sin and evil give you a bad feeling, this is, in itself, a very positive thing.[69]

DESPAIR

When a person is too hard on himself and dwells only on the bad, he may not see any good at all in his life, and this can cause despair.[70]

UNION WITH G-D

All t'shuva, even t'shuva motivated by a fear of punishment, ultimately stems from the desire to be united with G-d.[71]

PERSONAL PATHWAYS

Every Jew has his own specific pathway to t'shuva. General

68. 16:2.
69. 16:7.
70. Ibid.
71. 16:8.

t'shuvas will not suffice. Everyone has to find the path appropriate for his own unique soul, and his unique role in life.[72]

THE TORAH BLUES

Very often, when a person who lives life with great gusto approaches some holy act, all of a sudden he feels an overwhelming fatigue and heaviness. How is it that he is full of energy when it comes to secular things, and lethargic when it comes to Judaism and Torah?

When a person comes into contact with holiness, his soul is in a state of higher illumination. It perceives more clearly what absolute perfection involves. As a result, the person senses his own limitations and nothingness, and feels embittered toward the holy act or ideal which has caused these feelings. For instance, when a person sits down to learn Torah, he feels G-d's demands for morality; he senses man's great responsibility; he understands that man's every action is imbued with a life-and-death import. Opening the Talmud, he feels he is entering a project so cosmic that it is beyond his strength. He is pained and weakened by the unfathomable depth of the task.

Yet this very feeling is the foundation of t'shuva. Every person who feels overwhelmed as he approaches the commandments and Torah learning must know that this is a sign that he is deeply connected to them. Let him rejoice in his anguish and continue forward until his pain is replaced with a great holy pleasure.[73]

72. 16:10.
73. 16:5.

THE TWO PATHS ARE ONE

The foundation of higher t'shuva is a holy enlightenment and feeling a great delight in G-d. It is the t'shuva a person does to perfect his inner life, his thoughts, morals, and ideals. To do this, one must cleanse oneself of all the barriers distancing him from G-d, until he clings to G-d with all his might.

This inner search is hindered by the study of all the detailed laws, and by a preoccupation with their performance, because the deep meditation needed for this sublime purification is beyond concrete, specific acts.

In contrast, lower t'shuva is directed toward the world, to perfect one's actions and relationships with others. Here, a detailed knowledge of all of the laws is needed, followed by a course of action leading to their implementation. In this case, one's path can be hindered by the deeper meditation of higher t'shuva.

The two paths go together. Every step of higher t'shuva should elevate one's lower t'shuva, and every increase in worldly t'shuva should inspire additional forays of inner purification. Though the two paths seem to be at odds, they are really inseparable, like the body to the soul.[74]

RUNNING AND RETURNING

The higher t'shuva is the basis of the lower t'shuva, for without the lofty goal of reaching greater enlightenment, the

74.   16:11.

person on a path of lower t'shuva would not have the stamina and motivation to mend all of the details of behavior and disposition. If a person should occasionally feel that he cannot complete the demands of the lower path of t'shuva, let him run to the higher t'shuva. Ultimately, he will succeed, since his inner wish is to achieve both levels, and, in time, he will return from the higher t'shuva to bring holiness to every facet of his everyday life.[75]

NATIONAL SURVIVAL

For the nation's survival, we must awaken people to t'shuva. We need to be bonded together for our future. Our unity derives from our unique holy way of life and way of thinking. When we uphold our holy ways and thoughts, then our inner unity exists. However, with the weakening of our spirituality, disunity increases, and the fact of belonging to the same race, religion, country, and society will be unable to unite the many divisions and factions which form to deal with life's many demands.[76]

THE MASK OF EVIL

There are elite tzaddikim who perceive the whole world in a positive light. They see good in everything. In the clarity of their vision, they see how evil itself plays a positive role. They understand that the evil in the world is a screen which tempers the Divine light, so that it can illuminate the world, but the evil does not damage or destroy the light. They understand that the

75. 15:6.
76. 12:11.

pure light is far too great for the world to contain, and yet the light must shine. Therefore, there must be screens to lessen the light, and these screens are the evil in the world and its perpetrators.[77]

77.   16:12.

Chapter Twenty-One

THE ROAD TO PERFECTION

T'SHUVA WILL SURELY COME

"We are delayed on the road to perfection, and we avoid it because of an exaggerated fear which we experience when the idea of t'shuva confronts us. We remain immersed in pain and weakness from the melancholy which the thoughts of t'shuva awaken. For this reason, we reject the very thing which is the source of the happiness of all of our being, and we remain lost in the wilderness of life. This situation, however, cannot last. We must strengthen ourselves with spiritual boldness, with the power of t'shuva's song. All of its accompanying sorrow must be transformed into a vibrant song which revives, fortifies, comforts, and heals. Then we will experience t'shuva and all of its stages as a sweet and delightful whole, which will constantly fill up our thoughts, and we will order our lives in its light, for our personal wellbeing, and for the good of mankind, in this world and the next, for the redemption of the individual and all humanity, for the rebirth of the Jewish nation and its return from exile, forever, as in ancient days long past."[1]

1. *Orot HaT'shuva*, 17:6.

APPENDIX

T'SHUVA AND PEACE*

"Dear Brothers, those who are anguished over the pain of our nation and who feel with all of their souls its awful destruction, tribulation and disgrace – the truth is clear that no cure, nor easing of the frightening situation of the nation can possibly occur other than the return to the cradle of our youth, to the Holy Land, to build it and to be built up by it!

"The time has come that, from out of the quagmire of all our thoughts, we come to the conclusion and recognition that for once and for all time, the beginning and end of our national endeavor, which requires such great effort, such great talent, and so much self-sacrifice on all of our parts, these are all rooted in and welded together with the great key of redemption – t'shuva.

"However, there are many things which inhibit our t'shuva, and we are obligated to remove them from our midst and to

---

*   *Orot HaT'shuva*, Appendix, Ohr Etzion Edition, 7.

overcome them with all of our strength. The principal barrier, however, which truly contains all others within it, especially when speaking about the general t'shuva of all of the nation with all of its factions, in relation to the course of the emerging redemption which is developing and budding in our midst, this is the false picture of t'shuva as being something associated with a poverty of spirit, with weakness, feebleness and the strangulation of life. This picture also truly damages the t'shuva of every individual, as is widely known, but more than anything it obstructs the t'shuva of the nation, which is now destined to come at this time with the beginning traces of the redemption, with which we must be braced with strength and yearning to be satiated with the dew of life, with mighty creativity and vitality.

"And for this, we are obligated to reveal this secret, that the true t'shuva of all of the Jewish people – of which the return to the Land of Israel, which is continuing and increasing in our midst, is one of its greatest foundations – must be planted in our inner beings like a mighty, powerful vision, which gives us treasures of boldness and strength, to stand with a firm spirit against all of our oppressors, and to stir within us an exalted creative spirit, one which is dynamically growing with all of the spiritual and material values that we have in the valor of the Rock of Israel.

"This life-abounding t'shuva which flows not from individual downtrodden souls, but rather from the treasury of the soul of the entire nation of *Knesset Yisrael* which unifies within it all of its many different organs, this t'shuva comes to us through manifestations that can be divided into four eternal, absolute values which appear in a cognizant step-by-step fashion. These values are honor, love, knowledge, and life.

"Honor must return to us, the honor due to our people, the honor of the nation and all of its exalted, holy acquisitions, without allowing ourselves the habit of belittling any one of them.

"After honor comes love, for without honor (toward the nation in all of its aspects) an idealized love cannot find expression. Together with appearance of honor, the noble love (for our nation) immediately appears and sends us its rays.

"After love, knowledge must come – the banishment of ignorance (ignorance regarding our history, our religion, our heritage) must come speedily, engaging our attention all of the time.

"And all of these values will bring us life, the life of Judaism, complete in all of its wholeness.

"From t'shuva that is learned in this form, the light of peace will also flow to us with all of its glow.

"We have no party that you will not find within its midst a proper relation to at least one of these values. And from the living relationship to the one, the soul's inner striving toward completeness is prepared to link up the entire chain until its conclusion, and the soul of Israel in its wholeness will be ready to return to its great strength as in the days of yore.

"Listen please, my dear brothers, and place this golden key, the key of the true redemption – t'shuva – upon your heart. And a year of redemption and salvation, a year of peace and true brotherly love will befall us quickly in our days, Amen."

Index of *OROT HAT'SHUVA*
found in this volume